Keeping Current

*Advanced
Internet
Strategies
to Meet
Librarian and
Patron Needs*

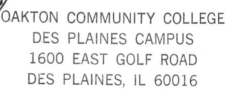

STEVEN M. COHEN

AMERICAN LIBRARY ASSOCIATION
Chicago   2003

While extensive effort has gone into ensuring the reliability of information appearing in this book, the publisher makes no warranty, express or implied, on the accuracy or reliability of the information, and does not assume and hereby disclaims any liability to any person for any loss or damage caused by errors or omissions in this publication.

Composition by ALA Editions in Bembo and Avant Garde in QuarkXPress 5.0 on a PC platform

Printed on 50-pound white offset, a pH–neutral stock, and printed on 10-point cover stock by McNaughton & Gunn

The paper used in this publication meets the minimum requirements of American National Standard for Information Sciences—Permanence of Paper for Printed Library Materials, ANSI Z39.48-1992. ∞

Library of Congress Cataloging-in-Publication Data

Cohen, Steven M., 1974-
 Keeping current : advanced Internet strategies to meet librarian and patron needs / Steven M. Cohen.
  p. cm.
 Includes index.
 Contents: Current developments in currency—Search engines—Web site monitoring software—Weblogs—RSS feeds.
 ISBN 0-8389-0864-0
 1. Current awareness services—Information technology. 2. Computer network resources—Management. 3. World Wide Web—Computer programs. 4. Web search engines. 5. Weblogs. 6. Library science—Computer network resources. 7. Communication in library science. I. Title.
ZA4201.C58 2004
025.5'25'02854678—dc21   2003013008

Printed in the United States of America

07 06 05 04 03   5 4 3 2 1

To Hallie Elizabeth Cohen

CONTENTS

FIGURES

ACKNOWLEDGMENTS

Since I wrote my first high school essay, I have always wanted to write a book, so when I was approached by Renée Vaillancourt McGrath to submit a proposal to ALA Editions, I was thrilled and ready for the challenge. In addition to the thrill of writing the book itself, I always looked forward to putting into words my thoughts and feelings on the people in my life who have helped me get this far in my career. This book could not have come about without the support from the following people:

Myron Roochvarg, Laurie Pastore, Edana Cichanowitz, Kathy Greco, Barbara Norcia, Jenny Levine, Gary Price, Genie Tyburski, Blake Carver, that guy at Circuit City, Dr. Barry Greenberg, Ronald and Christine Mehilentze, and Natalie and Paul Blacher.

The following deserve special mention:

Erwin and Sandy Cohen—for believing in my work as a library professional and always encouraging me to work harder and strive to be the best librarian, husband, and father that I could possibly be.

Barbie Cohen—for being my best friend. Words cannot express how I feel for her. She pushes me to be the best that I can possibly be and always encourages my work, even though I am up until the wee hours of the morning. She also locates my wallet, keys, cell phone, glasses, and every other essential item that I lose constantly.

Renée Vaillancourt McGrath and Eloise L. Kinney—for making what I wrote look better. This book definitely couldn't have been written without Renée, as she was the one who suggested that I write it. Her continued faith in my theories and ability to fix my fragmented sentences are always appreciated. Eloise helped copyedit the book, and the sentences flow because of her hard work.

INTRODUCTION

Do you keep current? Do you know what is happening in your profession? Are you able to keep up with the current events that fuel your patrons' reference questions? Or are you too overwhelmed by the glut of information in today's electronic world to even bother? Librarians need to keep current, and this book will show you how.

KEEPING CURRENT

Currency, in terms of library science, means keeping up with what is happening in the field and in our patrons' areas of interest. This book provides practical advice on how busy librarians can stay current while the Web keeps getting bigger and deeper. There are two reasons for librarians to keep current, as mentioned above: monitoring ongoing news and resources for their profession and locating useful resources for their patrons. Many of the essential tools that will be described in *Keeping Current* will help librarians stay current despite their busy work environments. Staying current can range from establishing membership on discussion lists and mailing lists to attending professional conferences (physically or virtually) to reading library-related weblogs.

Staying on top of current developments is often difficult, overwhelming, and cumbersome, but there are ways in which librarians can keep abreast using the latest technologies without falling victim to information overload. Without a guide, many librarians may feel overwhelmed by currency and abandon it altogether. Yet, to serve our customers better, librarians must not only embrace the Web, but also make it a goal to use it to its utmost capabilities. If librarians are able to show their patrons that they are hip and know and understand the current developments on the Web, they will be seen as cutting edge. Thus, the search engine will not replace the librarian; the librarian will become the search engine.

ACTUAL VIRTUAL CHAT SESSION
BETWEEN LIBRARIAN AND PATRON

> *Patron:* What is the inspiration for the song "New York State of Mind" by Billy Joel? I have searched the entire Web for three hours and have come up with nothing.
>
> *Live Librarian:* Hold on and I will try to find the answer for you.
>
> (Elapsed time—1 minute)
>
> *Live Librarian:* The other day, I was sent a web site called Songfacts (http://www.songfacts.com) via an electronic mailing list. I looked up that particular song and came up with this. I hope that it helps.
>
> *Patron:* Wow! That is perfect! Thanks!
>
> *Live Librarian:* Thank you for using Live Librarian.

The above online chat session took place one evening while I was working as a "Live Librarian," performing real-time reference work for patrons in my county. Was it a coincidence that I had seen Songfacts just a few days prior to this chat and thus could send such an immediate and timely response? Most would argue that this was indeed the case. I was a "lucky librarian." This happens all the time. By a sheer flip of the cybercoin, I just happened to log on to my e-mail and read a message on a discussion list that someone just happened to post. Congratulations Mr. "Live Librarian." You won't get so lucky next time.

In addition, accessing this particular site was not the only way to answer this particular question, yet the patron searched the Web for three hours and couldn't find the answer. Librarians who perform reference work have argued that patrons' Web-searching skills are not as extensive as they should be. My experience as a reference librarian both in a public library and in a large law firm library would prove this to be the case. Maybe the patron wasn't using the correct search terms, the appropriate Boolean logic required in many search engines, or even multiple search engines. A professional librarian would know how to find the answer to the "Billy Joel" query by using more in-depth search criteria, searching articles in professional databases, or even referring to (gasp!) print resources.

After the chat session, I performed thirty minutes of research on the "Billy Joel" query, using all aspects of reference work that have become part of my research repertoire, including advanced search techniques, multiple search engines, subject-specific directories, and many fee-based databases. Although I found information that would have been of use to the patron (such as interviews with Billy Joel that mention his work on "New York State of Mind"), Songfacts produced the most relevant results. Contrary to popular belief, not every answer can be found using Google.

So, was it a coincidence that I came across Songfacts a few days before this question appeared? Most would argue that this was indeed the case. I agree, in part, with this notion. I was half lucky. Many factors might have prevented me from looking at Songfacts before taking on this reference question. I could easily have skipped over the particular post that mentioned the site. Also, this message could have been posted a few days or weeks after the chat session with this patron (this has happened to me many times—the librarian equivalent of football's Monday morning quarterback).

On the other hand, why do librarians and information professionals subscribe to mailing lists? Most do so to communicate with other librarians across the world, run ideas by each other, ask for help on tough reference questions, and keep current with what is going on with librarianship as a whole. I subscribe to about three library- and Internet-related mailing lists, and the fact that I am on these lists increases the odds that I will be notified of a web site that could conceivably be used to answer a reference question.

Also, basic psychology suggests that the short lag between the time I saw Songfacts and when I was asked the "Billy Joel" question increased my chances of remembering the URL and its contents. However, even if the lag were greater, I still would have a high chance of recovering the site if I had placed it in an organized folder for future use. Many of us have bookmarks saved on our computers that have grown exponentially throughout the years, but we may lack the patience and time to place each web site into categorized folders. After viewing Songfacts, I determined that this site was worth saving for ready-reference purposes, so I would have been able to retrieve it even if the lag time was greater than it was.

Thus, even though the odds were in my favor for remembering a site that I needed to answer this particular question, the fact that I subscribe to particular mailing lists and organize the resources that I see on a daily basis worked in my favor. More important, I was able to provide quality reference service to a patron who, in turn, may recommend the program to his or her friends. So, luck was partially on my side in the reference chat center that evening, but the retrieval of Songfacts from memory could not have been accomplished at all if I had not actually seen the site in the first place.

FOR REFERENCE WORK

Librarians compete with the Internet on a daily basis. Keeping up-to-date with the latest web trends and reference sites, as well as news and topics related to librarianship, instills an edge of competitiveness with the ever-changing Web and the forces that are trying to take away our customers. I once saw a comic strip that showed a librarian sitting at the reference desk, and the plate that usually displays the name of the reference worker on duty simply said "Search Engine."

Although this comic could be construed as a jab at the library profession, I saw it as a wake-up call to all practicing librarians around the world. Consider this scenario: what if the ability to search the Internet was available only via the reference desk at every public and academic library? Everyone would have the capability to browse the Web at home without the use of any search engines, but only at the library reference desk could Google or Yahoo! be accessed. Imagine if the reference librarian was the search engine for the world's Internet users!

Consider these statistics recently released by the Pew Internet and American Life Project. Eight out of every 10 American Internet users use search engines to find information, and more than 33 million unique web users use search engines on any given day. In May 2002, 43 million people used the MSN search engine, 38 million searched Yahoo! and 36 million used Google. That is almost 100 million unique visitors to only three of the top search engines currently being used.[1]

Imagine all of these people walking into the library, calling on the telephone, or requesting searches via a live reference chat session. Would you be ready for the infinite amount of search queries (and the varying types of questions) that would be asked? Are you ready to become the "search engine" for your community? Sounds overwhelming, right? When you consider that only 15 to 20 percent of the Web is accessible via search resources, the job of "search engine" becomes more daunting.

Even though this scenario is not reality (libraries couldn't possible handle every search engine request), the old reference standard remains that, to coin a phrase from the 1994 blockbuster movie *Forrest Gump,* "You never know what you're gonna get." Each patron that reference workers interact with on a daily basis could come up with *any* query possible, from the sublime to the extraordinary, and because more and more reference queries are being answered using and via the Internet, it would make sense to know as much as possible about that medium. I am not advocating that every librarian know and analyze every web site in existence (an impossible task), but I do believe that librarians should do the best they can to keep current.

FOR PROFESSIONAL DEVELOPMENT

Consider another scenario, which is more likely to take place than the previous one. The board of trustees at your place of business (this could take place at a public library, university, law firm, school, etc.) has asked you to join them at their monthly meeting. You show up for the meeting dressed in your favorite suit or dress (this is the board of trustees), they greet you with a smile and a nod, and the meeting begins.

After going through the normal business activities, they turn their attention to you. The president notices that circulation has decreased exponentially over the past five years and is worried that their customers aren't using the library anymore. He has also noticed that, every year, your budget requests have been increasing despite this drop in circulation. Another member chimes in, mentioning that most of the people needing research are now doing it themselves over the Internet. They just have to go to Yahoo! type in what they want, and it comes right up. Why do we need a library?

This is not an entirely fictitious scenario. Sadly, librarians all over the country have to justify their existence daily, whether it is to patrons in the public library sector, the president of a private company, or a dean at a university. You know the drill and respond in typical librarian fashion: circulation numbers do not justify the type of work librarians do for their constituencies. Librarians have many other responsibilities, for example, training customers on the use of the Internet, negotiating with vendors on the use of proprietary databases, and answering reference questions. You also mention the statistics for the materials that patrons use in the library but do not check out. Customers, you relay, are taking advantage of the Borders and Barnes and Noble phenomenon. They browse the library stacks, sit at a table, and read books in the building.

The members of the board understand that but need more information. They want to know the state of libraries around the country. Are they having the same problems with circulation? How are these libraries justifying their existence to their members? What are they doing to attract customers? Have many libraries been closing or have more been opening?

A smile appears. Having just read an article in the *Christian Science Monitor* entitled "The Web Didn't Kill Libraries. It's the New Draw," you discuss that in the year 2001, more than $600 million was spent on U.S. library construction, an increase of 15 percent from ten years prior. That accounts for more than 80 new libraries and renovations on 132 new buildings. Most libraries need to get approval from their communities before they build and renovate their buildings; thus, patrons are valuing libraries across the country enough that they want to use their tax dollars to pay for them. If the board is still worried about circulation statistics, you mention the 1.7 billion items checked out of American libraries in 1999, a 21 percent increase from a decade prior.[2]

Regarding patrons' use of the Internet rather than using the library, you state that this is a big issue with library professionals all around the country. The problem, obviously, is reliable reference sources. Patrons, especially those in grade school, use any web site that they find as sources for their term papers and homework. Many times, these sources are not credible. (For example, there was the story that surfaced a few years ago in which a graduate student referenced a web site in an essay only to find out a few months later that it was the work of an eight-year-old.)

Librarians need to provide their customers with credible web sites from credible sources. There are two ways to do this. First, with the "who, what, where, when, why, and how" method, find out as much as possible about the site itself, the author, and the sources used to provide the information. Second, and more important, subscribe to electronic mailing lists that send out periodic e-mails listing ready-reference web sources that librarians can offer to their patrons. Such mailing lists include the Librarians Index to the Internet (http://www.lii.org) and Infomine (http://infomine.ucr.edu).

Patrons' misuse of search engines is a major problem that will continue to get worse as the Web gets bigger and the number of engines increases. As a librarian, you have firsthand knowledge that many patrons do not understand how to use these engines to their utmost capabilities. For example, many have never used the advanced search feature available on every engine. Second, you explain that only 15 to 20 percent of the content on the Web is accessible to the popular search engines. In fact, this problem is so prevalent that some librarians have dedicated their careers to finding these "hidden databases" and bringing them to the public. Third, many think that Yahoo! and Google are the "be all and end all" of the Web, and if patrons couldn't find what they are looking for using either one of these engines, then it doesn't exist. This is simply not true, and you proceed to discuss all of the newer engines that have come on the market in the past year alone.

The board is impressed with your vast knowledge of library awareness and Web usage and asks how you have obtained all of this current knowledge. In a fifteen-minute speech, you discuss all of the methods that you use to keep current (methods you will learn in this book!). The board president admits that he did not know any of the facts that were discussed and would like you to attend every meeting to keep the board informed about what is going on in the library and with web usage. You have impressed the board, but you have also taught them important information about the ever-changing world of the Internet. Now, how can you stay on top of the subject so that you are ready for every board meeting *and* every patron? *Keeping Current* can help.

ABOUT *KEEPING CURRENT*

Chapter 1 discusses the history of currency in library and information science, how currency has changed over the years, and why keeping current has become more difficult since the advent of the Web. Some would argue that before 1993, it was fairly easy to keep current. There were print publications, conferences, and regional workshops. In this chapter, I discuss how currency has changed since 1993, how it has affected the way we perform reference work, and how, although it may seem more difficult and time-consuming, in reality it is not. One of the ways librarians keep current is by simply reading the newspaper and watching the news, and a discussion on these tools ensues. This chapter also notes how the ways that librarians and information professionals kept current before the Web have not been abandoned but transformed into a digital medium.

Chapter 2 discusses search engines and lays out the importance of staying on top of the daily changes in the databases that are searched (when one uses search engines, the entire Web is not actually searched) and the search features in the engines themselves. As mentioned earlier, there are many search engines other than Google that could be used to supply different results, and these will be brought to the readers' attention. This chapter also includes a discussion of the Invisible Web (information from the Web that is not seen and picked up by the major search engines), which could encompass more than 60 percent of the full Internet. This chapter provides tools that are used to dig deeper into the Invisible Web and bring this information to light. Also discussed in this chapter are specialized news search engines.

Chapter 3 discusses web site monitoring software, which allows the user to keep up with multiple web sites on one piece of software. This saves time in that one need not go to each web site every day. If the site is updated, the user is notified via the software. Using web site monitoring software on the sites that one normally visits will cut down on the time used for professional development work on the Web.

One of the more recent phenomena that is just now beginning to hit mainstream web users is weblogs. Weblogs (or "blogs") are frequently updated web sites that provide links (usually, but not always, on a specific topic) to stories, articles, and other web sites, listed chronologically, with a discussion about each posting. Weblogs are different than home pages or personal web sites in that they can be updated easily using free or fee-based software. Chapter 4 provides a history of "blogging," the current state of blogs, and how they are used to keep current on a particular topic. Features of weblogs are mentioned along with a step-by-step process of setting one up, a discussion of the different software that can be used, and samples of resources used by bloggers to make their blogs more interactive. This chapter also provides blogs by librarians and information professionals and explains why blogs are the perfect tool for librarians to provide content to their constituencies and how they are also useful for professional development and reference work.

Chapter 5 focuses on RSS (Rich Site Summary or Really Simple Syndication) feeds, an even more recent aspect of providing content to users based on XML (Extensible Markup Language). This chapter does not focus on the technical side of RSS feeds but discusses the ways in which these feeds can be used to keep current and, more important, how librarians can save time while using them. RSS feeds allow for content to be pulled from any type of web site (i.e., news sites, weblogs, etc.) and then be "fed" into a piece of software known as a news aggregator (the different types of aggregators are discussed in this chapter). The aggregator then displays the content from these sites in one list, thus saving time by not necessitating a visit to each site. Instead of my going to two hundred sites every day that I use to stay current, the new content from these sites comes to my desktop. Tips on how to utilize RSS feeds effectively are discussed as well as how to find the feeds and "aggregate" them into a newsreader.

Throughout the course of this book, and during the discussions on the methods used to keep current in our field, I would like you to think about the ways that you keep up with new resources and news related to librarianship. Also, during the days or weeks that it takes for you to get to the end of *Keeping Current,* I would like you to time yourself on how long it takes for you to stay current. If it takes more than one hour per day, it is too long.

NOTES

1. Search Engines: A Pew Internet Project Data Memo, July 3, 2002, available at http://www.pewinternet.org/reports/toc.asp?Report=64.
2. Steve Fries, The Web didn't kill libraries. It's the new draw, *Christian Science Monitor,* July 25, 2002, available at http://www.csmonitor.com/2002/0725/p02s02-ussc.html.

Developments in Currency   1

Librarians have been keeping current ever since there has been information about which *to* keep current. Since the beginning of librarianship, information professionals have been networking with colleagues and attending conferences to learn how to make their jobs better and easier to perform. Over the years, there have been more methods available for currency that have been continuously used during any moment in time. Also, since the Web has become such an impressive tool, the features available lend themselves to currency and our quest to stay on top of our profession. Thus, a distinction exists between the ways that librarians kept current before electronic media became prevalent and after the burst of the Web.

The dividing line between keeping current using traditional methods and via the Web can be traced to the early to mid-1990s, when the Web started to become a viable tool for librarians to answer reference questions and for professional development purposes. The Web truly changed the way that information professionals performed their jobs and continues to change as the twenty-first century progresses. Within the scope of this book, with currency as its theme, electronic media has been the force that allows librarians to foster a comprehensive approach to currency.

The advent of the Web definitely has had an effect on how we keep current and is mentioned in detail in this chapter. Also, in what may seem a contradiction, the online media has had deleterious effects on currency. This contradiction is a theme throughout the book (in fact, without it, this book need not be written) and is the force for the theories portrayed and advice given.

As this chapter points out, print media still has its place in the profession in regard to keeping current. Other ways that librarians kept current before the Web will also be discussed because of their vitality throughout the years despite the attraction of online media. The differences between print and electronic tools for currency are discussed in this chapter, as are the pros and cons of each.

The last part of this chapter includes my theory on how currency can help the information professional to gain an edge over any competition as well as to become more aware of professional development aspects of the job. One part of my theory is that to serve our patrons well in the area of reference work, we need to be up-to-speed on many areas of the Web, most notably, search engines. Even so, keeping current need not be a time-consuming activity and can usually be accomplished within an hour per day. The time will be well spent and should improve the way librarians serve their constituencies.

CURRENCY BEFORE THE WEB

Think back to before you had your first e-mail account, before you were able to attempt to gain the answer to many a question by using a search engine, before the Internet was available. It was a time when an encyclopedia was the method of choice for answering a simple reference question, a time when direct communication was only available via the telephone or in person. How did you keep up with the changing times in librarianship? What were the methods for staying current with new reference materials or news in the library and information science field?

Trade journals have been used by librarians for a very long time and have consistently provided avenues for currency via news releases, feature articles, book reviews, and editorials. Before the modern Web, these trade journals could have been one of only two methods used to keep tabs on the profession. Librarians in record numbers still subscribe to *Library Journal, American Libraries,* and the other subdivision magazines and newsletters that have sprung up throughout the years.

Another method of currency used by librarians before the Web includes attending conferences, either national conferences sponsored by the American Library Association or regional, state, or county gatherings. Just as the major trade journals led to division publications, the national conferences also helped to create more focused conferences, typically geared toward a specific type of librarianship, such as public libraries. As the Web became a force in information science, even more trade journals and conferences began to appear.

A lot has been said about reading the newspaper as a method of currency for reference work. When I was a librarian trainee at a public library, I would make it a point to read *Newsday* and the *New York Times* during my break to catch up on the news topics of the past day. When 3:00 P.M. rolled around, there would always be at least one student who had to write a paper on a current-event topic. I would then be able to point to a news feature in the paper as a starting point for the research. It is important not to underestimate the power of the local newspapers as well. Reading the local paper has helped both my work in public libraries and in my current position in a law library.

In the public library sector, reading the local community papers will enable the reference staff to interact with patrons on the topics that directly affect them. For example, senior citizens are notorious for striking up conversations with the front-end staff. Also, students are assigned projects that deal with the history or current events of the local community. By reading up on these local issues, the information professional can get a head start on the assignments that are to come, collect articles that appear in these papers, and be seen as one who is knowledgeable about local and regional information.

This same theory works well in the law library (or in any special library). Many high-end executives are on the boards of local nonprofit organizations and like to see information that comes out of local newspapers dealing with them. It is human nature to like seeing our names in the paper. Librarians can act as a clipping service by reading the local papers in which their patrons' names will more likely appear. Providing this content to the customers before they ask for it shows initiative and also does wonders for the public relations for the library. Many newspapers can be read online now, but the smaller publications have been slower to get on the Web. Thus, this method of currency that was started long before the Web still thrives today.

Before the Web became what it is today—with its numerous tools used for currency—electronic mailing lists, Usenet, and e-mail were used by librarians to network with colleagues for reference and professional development needs. I remember working in a public library as a high school student in 1991 and 1992 and becoming fascinated with a librarian who was using the Stumpers electronic discussion list to both ask questions and provide help to those in need. I was amazed that one could communicate with other professionals in an electronic environment, sharing ideas and gaining knowledge, and have fun while doing it. Although these tools are considered to be the earliest aspects of the public Web, librarians still use discussion lists (although not as much Usenet) to communicate with their colleagues. In fact, the electronic mailing list is probably one of the easiest and cheapest methods for currency despite its veteran status. The cliché "The more things change, the more they stay the same" is perfect in this instance.

One of the issues that consistently arises when dealing with currency is that there is too much information out there to keep up. Before the Web existed as we know it today, there was less content, and it was conceivable to keep up without having other work suffer as a result. Every now and then a trade journal would come across the reference desk, and regional and national conferences were attended at high numbers, but that was only a fraction of the amount of content available today via the Web. Not only that, but the Web has inspired the onset of print publications whose content discusses, of course, the "information superhighway" and all that can be seen on it. As the technologies improve, as we delve more into how the Web can help us perform our jobs better, how we can communicate easier with colleagues, how message boards make professional development so successful, some may pine for the days when there were only two or three trade journals worth reading. On the other hand, these are exciting times we live in. We just need to strike a balance.

HOW THE WEB HAS CHANGED CURRENCY

Although print media has its place in the currency of any profession, one would be remiss to deny the effect of the Web on day-to-day work practices. With the amount of information available, some predict that in the future books will be nonexistent (a theory despised and criticized by librarians, and rightly so). Although an all-or-nothing approach should not be taken in such an important matter, the Web does have its positive aspects regarding currency, especially for the information professional.

The number of tools for currency that are available on the Web is staggering. These tools provide the user with a constant flow of information that can be manipulated to suit the needs of even more users—namely, the customers we serve on a daily basis or our professional colleagues. Such tools as web site monitoring devices, weblogs, and RSS (Rich Site Summary or Really Simple Syndication) feeds will be discussed at length in the remaining chapters of this book. Built by those who have been working on the Web for many years, these tools have developed a reputation of usability and keep improving with every new release. Compare these extraordinary tools with any print media. Although reference books have changed over the years to suit our needs better, they are still one-dimensional when placed side by side with the wonders of the Web.

Workshops and conferences have also become part of the Web environment. Not only is the Web being discussed at length in record numbers at these gatherings, but the actual presentations can be viewed online within hours of them happening. Although video and audio via the Web have not garnered as much attention as they should, the possibility of virtually "attending" a conference while sitting at your desk has many advantages, financial being the most obvious. Also, the slides used during the talks are usually available online within a few weeks after the conferences, which allows readers to "participate" even though they are not actually physically present. Before the Web, one would have to get a copy of the proceedings or talk to someone who attended, if available, to find out what went on during any particular session.

Information is constantly changing, and the Web has the buffers necessary to deal with these changes that only newspapers can match, but not that proficiently. With the power to publish and be read by millions of people at such a cheap price, the Web is unstoppable when it comes to current information, the key to the librarian attempting to stay one step ahead of his or her patrons. The short time needed to publish on the Web has been enhanced by the use of weblogs, online diaries that make maintaining and posting new material cheap and easy.

Let's look at technology from a purely democratic point of view. I was once taught that to fully understand one's point of view on any issue, the other side must also be researched thoroughly. With the Web as a tool for currency, one can do just that. The Web makes it easy to read about similar subjects from other points of view. There are many print reference guides that allow students to research both sides of every issue. Consider the Web as an advantage that provides these viewpoints for truly current events. This topic will be taken up more in chapter 4, on weblogs.

Although the above may be true, the Web has affected currency in detrimental ways also. Believe it or not, although the Web is probably the most effective tool to exist in the work of librarianship in the past half century, there are many problems associated with it, especially when it is used to stay focused and keep up-to-date.

First, and most obvious, there is too much content available online. Information overload has been a problem since everyone began to publish on the Web, and many have speculated that this could have the potential to back-fire and cause fewer people to use online services to locate answers to queries. Within the subject of keeping current, information overload is definitely an issue that needs to be addressed. How does the librarian keep current without suffering from the chronic illness that affects us all at some point in our career: too much of it at one time?

With this enormous amount of information to sift through, time becomes a factor. If we thought that we were too busy at work before online services became available, we must be drowning today. Time is of the essence in today's world, and keeping current can use up a lot of time, but, thankfully, it doesn't have to. Using the right tools properly, one can stay abreast with new ready-reference tools and professional development news in less than one hour per day. The remaining chapters focus on how this can be accom-plished.

Although information professionals can use the Web to stay current, they also need to keep up with new technologies. With print resources, there is only one medium, the book, and the technologies behind it haven't changed much throughout the years. With the Web, one needs to keep a constant eye out for developing technologies and how they can affect keeping current. As carpenters know, and as readers will see, keeping abreast also involves choos-ing the best tools for the job. Sometimes the tool is brand new, but it could be the next "big thing," which could, overall, decrease the amount of time spent keeping current. A complete circle develops. As an example, before I started keeping up with the technology for currency purposes, I spent at least three hours per day reading news articles, trade publications, and reviewing online resources. After finding and using the tools mentioned in this book, I have shaved that time by two-thirds. Thus, I am doing the same amount of reading in less time.

Along the lines of finding and using the most useful technological tools for your needs, librarians also need to stay abreast of new resources that will point them to further resources. Even though this may seem to be more time-consuming (more sites mean more time spent reading), it is truly important in terms of getting the best data available on the Web. With information over-load always a factor, finding these new sources may be harder than realized. As noted, librarians need to balance the amount of data gathered with time. Too many sources can yield an overload of data (which also involves a high number of crossover—repeated information from multiple sources). When adding new sources to the repertoire, information professionals should use the skills taught in library school in terms of analyzing material for validity. This for online ready-reference materials, but it should also be noted when using sources for professional development purposes. Sure, time needs to be put in when analyzing resources, but it is well worth it in this context.

One detrimental aspect of using online services for currency is the lack of human connection. I have always believed that librarianship cannot be performed in a vacuum. We need other professionals for ideas, validation, and sometimes materials via interlibrary loan. The same is true for keeping current. We attend conferences and regional meetings for the interaction and conversation and to get out of our libraries (a necessity in any profession) every once in a while, which online media does not facilitate (if anything, it hinders this process). At times, one can find more resources and news in the library world by talking with colleagues over a cup of coffee at a break in a meeting than via e-mail newsletters and the Web. That said, conference presentations are becoming more accessible online (following theories of distant learning), but nothing, in my opinion, can be more valuable in a learning environment than physically being present. When librarians first learned about performing a reference interview, we were told to use the body language and facial expressions of the patron asking the query and feed off of them. This can only be done in a face-to-face exchange.

Finally, the Web is distracting. With one click, we can be taken off course, and oftentimes, we forget why we turned on the computer in the first place! With currency, this can be extremely difficult in that we are sometimes brought to information that is not useful and needs to be filtered out manually (because the electronic filters we put in place, discussed throughout *Keeping Current*, did not work). Like all Web users, having a lot of information at our fingertips only breeds the higher probability of taking us away from the task at hand. With print resources, the likelihood of distraction probably diminishes. When reading a trade journal, the only distraction may come in the form of reference questions. If you are lucky enough to have "off-the-floor" time, then distractions are almost nonexistent. Compare the last time you read a full article online with the last time you read a full article in print. My guess is that you were able to finish the print article faster. There were fewer distractions.

PRINT VERSUS ELECTRONIC RESOURCES

The print versus electronic resources discussion is commonplace among librarians. Usually, this conversation revolves around whether to continue comes out on CD–ROM or whether to subscribe to both the online and print versions. Most of the time, this decision has a monetary factor involved. Is the cost of the publication worth it, considering the frequency of use? Regarding currency, there are aspects of print and electronic formats that appeal to the user and detriments as well. Some of the material for keeping current is only available in one format (either electronic or print), but a detailed discussion of the pros and cons of both formats will help the user decide which will work best for what purpose.

PRINT PROS

Trade publications, the most common way that librarians stay abreast of the profession, arrive like clockwork at the beginning of each month or every other week. It is a rare occasion that one of the "big two" *(American Libraries* and *Library Journal)* are delayed in publication. Professional editors, writers, and other specialists work so that each issue is filled with useful information that will help their readers stay up-to-date with current information science theories, job openings, book reviews, and a plethora of other projects. These publications have been around for a long time and have been able to withstand the bombardment of other media that take up time in the day of a busy librarian. They are viewed as a must read for every information professional and continue to be distributed throughout the library. In a library where I once worked, librarians would sometimes mark off sections of interest for others to read (my director also insisted that certain sections be read). These trade journals have become like Linus's security blanket in the Peanut's cartoon. We know that even though they may not always be around, we relish the fact that they exist.

Print publications can be taken everywhere. I carry around the current issues of four professional journals in my briefcase so that when I get a spare moment, I am able to pick one up and read it. The journals can also be stored on my desk or in a drawer for easy access when needed. There is no need to "log on" to any system, remember any passwords, or install any software to read them. For those who need to perform catch-up work at home, having the journals on hand is a relatively painless experience. Trade publications are very flexible as well and can withstand coffee spills, dog bites, and the like.

Trade publications have a professional feel to them. They come from reputable sources that have been in this business for a long period of time. If any article appears in these publications, the reader knows that it has been meticulously researched, drafted, edited, and looked over many times to make sure that the information provided is of top-notch quality. When being cited, the publications are easily recognized by readers and are available in almost all libraries. Even lesser-known publications in librarianship appear to the user as valid resources to peruse. When I was in library school, I used to relish walking through the professional publications section of the library, picking out a few journals, and reading them in a corner cubby. I felt like a true professional, a feeling that any online service can't touch.

Sometimes print media is the only option for reading an article in full text. Many companies that have been putting out relevant print magazines over the past decade have been forced to put some of their articles online because of reader demand but still retain other written work solely in print format (to maintain subscriptions). Thus, although big organizations, associations, and companies that own these magazines continue to be the leading force and put out highly respected material, the print media will still be available.

PRINT CONS

The most valid point when discussing print media in relation to currency is the time factor. Although trade journals are mailed to subscribers every month or biweekly, and contain news items that they consider to be up-to-speed, there is a good chance that more information has become available on any particular story. The professional print media can't keep up with our quickly changing world, especially in an electronic era, where the demand from our customers is escalated because of their heightened expectations.

Another factor that weighs against print media is availability. Those librarians who do not subscribe to trade journals or do not get them routed at work and want to keep current using print methods need to become patrons of libraries themselves. Here, they go through the same trials and tribulations as the patrons in the institutions for which they work. Copies of the journal may be missing, the most current copy may not be allowed beyond the reference room, and, in an ironic twist, it may be circulating among the reference staff. Librarians who attempt to save money by looking elsewhere for library-related print material may be forced to waste time actually looking for it, which eventually causes too much frustration to consider journals to be handy tools.

We are all aware of the routing systems that are put into place at libraries, where print publications are sent around to the library staff for perusal before getting placed in the periodical stacks. Newer librarians, many just out of library school, may be very low in the hierarchical distribution chain and not see a new publication until weeks or even months after it is published. Many factors can contribute to this: a staff member is too busy to look through the magazine and places it aside to be read at a future date, a staff member is on vacation and these publications are piling up on her desk, or there are too many staff members and not enough subscriptions to go around.

The latter is a common occurrence at the law library where I am currently employed. We have more than fifteen subscriptions to a daily legal newspaper, and these publications get routed to more than one hundred attorneys. Attorneys can get very busy, do not have the time to read through the newspaper, and sometimes do not pass it on to the next person. One broken link in the routing chain can cause disaster to those underneath. I have had first-year associates who do not even read one particular publication because by the time they have it in their hands, it could be three or four weeks out of date, and the information is deemed useless. Although this is not necessarily true (any article is worthwhile if it pertains to a subject of interest), newer attorneys, who are in greater need of currency than veteran lawyers, give up on using print media and rely solely on online resources.

The cost factor also comes into play when dealing with currency using print resources. Subscriptions to journals sometimes come out of the library budget and not out of the wallet of the individual. But, for those who aren't employed at a library, and may not have access to a library (or choose not to use one), the cost of the journals may be too much to handle.

ELECTRONIC PROS

There are obvious benefits of using the Web for currency: up-to-the-minute information, the availability of the data, the 24/7 access, and the ease of communication between professionals.

The Web can provide the most current information available. As soon as a story becomes breaking news, it can be placed on a web site for the entire world to read. The events of September 11, 2001, are a fine example of this. As soon as the World Trade Center was hit, web sites from all over were putting up pictures and breaking news on the story. Radio and television were doing the same, but if traditional media were not readily available, then the Web sufficed. With currency in librarianship, late-breaking news may not be as important (I have yet to come across a news release that was a "life-or-death situation" when dealing with our profession), but the fact that the information is readily available is comforting.

Of greater importance to the librarian is the availability of the data on the Web. Before the Internet, if one wanted to read an article in a newspaper on the day of publication (especially one from another county or state), one would have to find a library that carried the material and hope that the article would be able to be retrieved and sent over. It is also possible that before electronic media became so ingrained, we would not have known about articles that appeared in publications outside of our local area.

The availability of articles that appear in the web-based versions of popular trade publications is another way that electronic media is effective. As mentioned above, it may take some time for these publications to make their way through the number of librarians reading them on a routing list. But some articles from these publications are simultaneously published on the company's web site. Thus, librarians need not wait to read current material. It should also be noted that not all full-text articles appear on the site for free, as the publisher would have no financial gain for doing so.

In some instances, librarians need not keep current during the hours that they are physically in the library building. For those who like to work at home (or have to), online access is available twenty-four hours per day (that is, if Internet access is available from home). In some instances, librarians can log on to the fee-based databases and read the professional literature that is available. Having access to material whenever possible allows librarians to keep current when it's convenient, increasing the chances that they will do it.

Finally, the Web increases communication between professionals. Putting e-mail aside, online forums are becoming very popular among librarians (*see* Between the Stacks—http://www.betweenthestacks.com). These web-based discussion forums allow librarians to interact with other librarians to discuss the hot topics affecting our profession.

ELECTRONIC CONS

The downsides of using electronic media for currency are plentiful and include the credibility of resources, the less-than-stellar act of maintaining a live Internet connection, information overload, and the money involved.

Librarians were taught in library school to always relay to the patron which resource was used to answer a reference question. This is done so that the patron can refer back to that publication, but also to show the patron that the resource is credible. With the Web, credibility can be an important factor when dealing with currency, and the librarian should be aware of the information's source. Because anyone can publish any type of data online without having to be an "expert" in the field, and with publishing technology becoming easier and easier to use, the job of the "credibility police" will become tougher and tougher. Librarians have to be more stringent in deciding where they glean their data from and which sites they read to get updated on new web sites for both reference work and professional reading.

Has the following ever happened to you? You are diligently working on a reference question or reading an article online, and all of a sudden, your connection seems to be slow or nonexistent. The confused looks on your colleagues' faces mirror yours as small chatter starts to emit from others at the desk. Has the Internet connection gone down? You then receive an e-mail from the IT Department in your building stating that there are problems with the fractional T1 line coming out of the service provider and that they are working on the problem and should have the system back up in a few hours.

A few hours? Your confusion turns into trepidation as you realize that a line has formed in front of the desk because patrons who have been working diligently at the public access terminals want to know what the problem is, and they have papers due in the morning. You curse yourself for not using the print media more often as your colleagues struggle with similar feelings.

The point of the above scenario is not only to remind readers of the vast print collection that goes underutilized in many libraries across the nation, but also to point out that sometimes electronic media is inaccessible to the user. This is more important to the practicing librarian when dealing in reference work than professional development (as mentioned, reading professional material two days after it is published will not affect a librarian's job), but it may remind information professionals not to fully rely on electronic media in any aspect of their job.

Another aspect of the Web that can be detrimental in our work involves the expectations that we have of online media. Our patrons have become so ingrained in the thought that they can get anything with the click of a mouse that they do not realize that not every article is available via electronic media, and sometimes document delivery or interlibrary loan is necessary. Librarians often have the same expectations. They may want to read an article that appeared in *American Libraries* and wonder why they can't find it on the public Web. A false sense of how much information is actually on the Web may lead the librarian to not consult print media for currency needs, which, in turn, would open the chances of missing an important article.

STEVEN'S THEORY OF CURRENCY

Taking into consideration all of the points mentioned in this chapter, I have come up with my own ideas as to how currency can be maintained without sacrificing time while still retrieving all of the information needed to form a well-established knowledge of librarianship and our new reference tools. I use these methods on a daily basis and have concluded that although they may work well in theory, there will always be hindrances to being completely up-to-date on all fronts. Work can get out of hand at the reference desk, reports need to be written, programs need to be provided to patrons, collections need to be developed, and there are other random library-related issues that need to be taken care of on a daily basis.

That said, the purpose of *Keeping Current* is to make the "keeping-up" process easier and less time-consuming. Using the methods discussed throughout each chapter, I have shaved off at least three hours per day of the time that I spend to keep current. It only takes about forty-five minutes for me to keep abreast of new reference sources and professional development material (which entails a perusal of about four hundred sources).

Librarians should not have to focus on "finding" material to keep current. Every article, journal, or resource will come to them either via a certain piece of software, e-mail alert, or electronic discussion list. By this I also mean librarians should not have to go to any web sites directly to read about any new features. You may be pointed to new data but will never have to go to a web site without any rhyme or reason for doing so. If you are not prompted, don't go. The information will come to you. Although that may sound counterproductive, it is not. It is my belief that librarians waste too much time going to web sites to find new information. When answering a reference query, we perform research, which is different from keeping current. There is no reason to research currency. Currency will come to us.

Second, keeping current should not take all day. Many librarians get bogged down using resources that do not provide any valid information for their needs. Either they are too lazy to delete these sites from their retrieval method of choice or they honestly feel that visiting these sites is helping, when the sources haven't produced any worthwhile resources in a long time. Librarians need to purge sites that continuously underperform. The longer it takes to read new material, the less time we can be spending on other work, such as tending to the needs of our patrons. I once saw a commercial for an online service whose whole premise in selling a faster Internet connection was "log on, do work, get out." A perfect analogy when dealing with currency.

Third, use as few tools as possible. This book describes many methods of keeping current, and they all have their advantages and disadvantages. Librarians need to weigh the advantages of using one method over another. Whichever one is chosen, it is important not to get bogged down in using more than two methods of currency (not including e-mail), as using too many tools can become a burden on time. Two methods are plenty, considering that one piece of software may not be able to handle all of the sites that one is attempting to monitor.

There is also the work-home dilemma that becomes an issue when dealing with software that needs to be downloaded. It is difficult to keep the same information on two pieces of software if working both from home and the office. One may have to continuously transfer information between the two computers, which becomes burdensome. Web-based tools, if they are available, come in handy and should be considered as the medium of choice for the work-home environment.

Finally, learning to skim headlines is beneficial when dealing with currency. There will be a lot of information coming across the screen or page, and the material needs to be skimmed for relevancy. If the headline looks promising, then the first few paragraphs should be consumed. At that point, the gist of the article should be apparent, and the reader can decide whether to pursue the article to the end.

Despite the efforts to keep current and the variety of manual and electronic filtering tools available, information professionals may find themselves unable to keep up. The one true answer to this problem is to rid oneself of a few materials that may not be as important. The librarian who is bogged down in professional reading is attempting to read too much. Becoming bogged down will only hinder the process, and the librarian may abandon it altogether. This is a bad idea. Currency is too important to not do it at all. The rest of this book should help shorten the time needed for keeping abreast of trends in the ever-changing world of librarianship.

Search Engines 2

Keeping up with search engine news is crucial to performing our best work online, because most of the work we do on the Web uses search engines. Also, many librarians teach Web courses at their public or university library, while those in the private sector show their customers how to use engines on a daily basis.

As the Web gets older and more complex, and more sites are added to the already vast number already in existence, the search technology that is used to both gather and distribute these sites needs to grow more extensive and become smarter. Newer engines are making their way on the market, declaring that they index more sites and provide better and easier ways for users to search the Web. New search technology may provide new ways for users to search web databases as well as provide new sources for the searcher. But, because there are so many "new engines," it is important to know how to evaluate them, so as to distill the relevant from the irrelevant.

The search engine is only as good as the user in front of it. Many do not use the advanced features that can be very helpful when performing a complex search. In addition, some search engines use truncation; many others do not. Besides the search queries that are used, the advanced features on many of the popular engines also provide better schemas that are rarely utilized by nonresearchers.

In addition, search engines come and go. Some engines provide hits based on the amount of money paid per click result, in which the site owner pays the search engine for a prominent listing. Engines that did not provide fee-based results may provide them now, and others may have ceased this type of

15

moneymaking operation (although this is rare). Librarians need to know about these pay-per-click engines to notify their customers that although the hit may have topped the list of search results, it may not be the most valid or useful.

This chapter discusses the major search engines and how librarians and other information professionals can keep up with this aspect of librarianship, but it is also important to keep abreast of the data and information that search engines are not able to add to their indexes because they remain hidden from their crawling software (also known as robots). Most commonly known as the Invisible Web, these databases are the hardest to find because the user has to take extra steps to find the information buried in them—steps that most users will not take.

The major search engines also offer subject-specific search capabilities in their engines, from news to pictures. There are also engines that focus only on providing one particular type of data. News engines will be discussed later in this chapter.

RESOURCES FOR KEEPING CURRENT

When I first started library school, in 1998, I took a class on database searching that included instruction on fee-based applications such as Lexis Nexis as well as the free public web search engines. During the first minute of our discussion on the free engines, the professor told the class to subscribe to the Search Engine Watch monthly newsletter entitled Search Engine Report, put out by Chris Sherman. It was the first search newsletter that I subscribed to, and I still consider it to be the best.

Search Engine Report (SER) (http://www.searchenginewatch.com/sereport/) provides an overview of the important happenings with engines from the past month. The articles are detailed, and the information is extremely helpful and insightful. At the end of every posting, Sherman points the readers to relevant web sites for further investigation.

SER is not free (a one-year membership is $90), but those who do not like paying for web content can subscribe to a "toned-down" version of the newsletter at no cost.

While SER provides a monthly review of the search engine world, the timelier newsletter Search Day (SD) (http://www.searchenginewatch.com/searchday/) is published daily. Also authored by Sherman, SD includes breaking news on search engines, an in-depth look into new engines or databases, and a commentary from Sherman or a guest author. Included in every edition of SD are search engine headlines from Moreover (http://www.moreover.com), discussed in more detail below. Both SER and SD are worth subscribing to.

Resourceshelf (http://www.resourceshelf.com) is a weblog created and maintained by Gary Price. Price is well known for his famous Price's Lists of Lists, which has evolved over the years into one of the most useful resources for reference work. Price's List of Lists (http://www.specialissues.com/lol/) was created in 1998 to be a repository of lists that have appeared on many web magazines. Similar to *The Book of Lists*, found on many a reference shelf, this resource is extremely helpful for those looking for any type of list. One can browse by subject or by magazine (http://www.specialissues.com/lol/displolmagazines.cfm). In the beginning of 2001, Price turned his vast knowledge of search engines (and much more) into Resourceshelf. Every day, Price posts articles, press releases, and web sites (usually before everyone else finds out) for his vast readership.

Included in his weblog are the "Web Resources of the Week," where Price discusses in detail a new search resource or any other major searching tool. Price also enjoys discussing major news in the search engine industry and does it at a fevered pace. Before posting on any story or new search feature, he will test out the new feature and will always be honest with his readers. Still into his list making, Price will also post numerous bibliographies and "top-ten" accounts on any major theme, be it top law firms or hospitals. In fact, he still maintains his lists, and they are listed (of course they would be) on the left side of the weblog.

Resourceshelf also has a free weekly mailing list, which Price calls his "tickler." Sent out every Thursday, the newsletter includes numerous postings (but not all) from the previous week. Recently, Resourceshelf has entered into the world of RSS (Rich Site Summary or Really Simple Syndication) feeds (discussed in chapter 5), which allow his posts to be seen via a news aggregator. This site should be reviewed daily.

Search Engine Showdown (SES) (http://www.searchengineshowdown.com) is not necessarily a current-awareness tool in the search engine arena. Rather, the contents of this site involve a deep and statistical analysis of the most popular engines on the market today. Greg Notess, the guru behind this site, investigates the inner workings of these engines, provides charts of the results, and writes an in-depth essay on these results.

Notess also provides charts on almost all aspects of search engines, such as which Boolean terms are accepted, whether truncation is allowed, and what fields can be searched (the results can only be in the title or URL of the page). A detailed review of most of the major players in search engines is also available. For any questions on searching a particular engine, users should consult Search Engine Showdown. The site also discusses, in detail, subject-specific engines, such as news engines and telephone directories.

As mentioned, the news section is not the strength of the site, but it will notify the user as to any new reports that are added and offer a commentary on the important events that searchers need to know about.

Pandia (http://www.pandia.com) is an all-encompassing search engine portal that includes, among other tools, a guide to web searching and articles and columns on the top search engines used today. Much of the information on Pandia deals with search engine optimization, an analysis of the way web sites are made and the way that engines enable top placement in the results listings based on fees or other factors.

The user should take a long look at Pandia before dismissing it as a marketplace for fee-based search engines. There is a lot of content that can be used to keep current, the most important aspect being the Search Engine Weblog (http://www.pandia.com/searchworld/index.html). Almost daily, this site provides its readers with search engine news as it relates to the professional searcher as well as to Webmasters who build sites. Within these postings are articles by Pandia reporters that provide more in-depth coverage of the current news (Pandia offers an e-mail subscription service that sends out a notice when a new article has been posted). There is also an extensive list of other resources, broken down by subject, that helps the end user keep up-to-date, as well as more current search engine news, pulled directly from Moreover. Finally, this search engine portal also provides extensive tutorials on searching the Web (http://www.pandia.com/web-searching.html), subject-specific search tools created by the Pandia Webmasters (http://www.pandia.com/search-tools.html), and an All-in-One page (http://www.pandia.com/all-in-one.html), which brings together almost everything on the other pages into one convenient spot. Spend some time at Pandia, and you are guaranteed to leave with at least five new search engine resources.

ResearchBuzz (http://www.researchbuzz.com), created and maintained by Tara Calishain, provides an informal, almost daily account of various search engine themes. She provides this information in a way that everyone will understand it, without being bogged down in web jargon. Whether it's a review of a directory on Beer Festivals (http://www.researchbuzz.com/news/2002/aug22aug2802.shtml#beerfestivals) or a discussion on a search engine tool (http://www.researchbuzz.com/news/2002/aug1aug702.shtml#googleteaming), Calishain not only finds it, but also spends a lot of time experimenting and looking around so that the user doesn't have to. For the lighter side of the news, Calishain gives us the Knickknack Drawer (http://www.researchbuzz.com/kdrawer/), random URLs that are fun and enjoyable but just don't fit into the ResearchBuzz mind frame. At times, although not as often as fans would like, Calishain provides lengthy articles on a research topic of her choosing.

To help readers keep up with the numerous writings posted on ResearchBuzz, there is a free mailing list; for those who don't mind the $30 fee ($20 for educators), a more extensive mailing list, ResearchBuzz Extra (http://www.researchbuzz.com/rbuzzextra.html), is also available.

One other note about ResearchBuzz. After the tragic events of September 11, 2001, Calishain began to collect numerous web resources about all aspects of that day. As of this writing, she continues to update her index (http://www.researchbuzz.com/911/index.html) and weblog for 9/11 news via a weblog (http://www.researchbuzz.com/911/mtype/) attached to the ResearchBuzz page. ResearchBuzz should be visited daily.

Search Engine Guide (SEG) (http://www.searchengineguide.com), similar to Pandia in its scope and versatility, is another site to use for keeping current. Much of the site deals with search engine marketing and optimization (important information for Webmasters but not necessarily for day-to-day librarianship and reference work), but two aspects of the site are particularly worth using.

First, the directory of more than three thousand subject-specific engines (http://www.searchengineguide.com/searchengines.html) is helpful when the major search engines are not providing the right answers. Sometimes it's better to narrow down the source to a topical directory of search features. This directory is broken down into subcategories, and all of the links are annotated (a must for any librarian). There is also a section entitled "What's New," which addresses the new search engines and directories that have been added.

Second, and more important, is the free daily e-mail newsletter that provides up-to-date news on all aspects of the search engine industry. Because SEG also markets itself as all encompassing, sometimes the user has to sift through numerous postings to get to the useful information, but it is well worth it.

Free Pint (http://www.freepint.com) is another free e-mail newsletter, delivered every two weeks, filled with information for the serious web searcher. Run by William Hann in the United Kingdom, this is one newsletter that should be read immediately after it reaches your inbox. Each issue features the following: an editorial from Hann, "My Favorite Tipples" (a brief listing of annotated links by library and information science professionals); the "Tips Article" (not present in every issue, this is one of two lengthy pieces in the newsletter focusing on web resources on a chosen subject); "The Free Pint Bookshelf" (a review of books related to libraries and information science); and the feature article (a lengthy piece enhancing the way we use and search the Web). The Free Pint newsletter has been running strong since 1997, and the full text of each issue is saved in the archives. There is also a topic archive so users looking for specific information can quickly locate articles that feature related content.

The newsletter is not the only feature in Free Pint. There is a job board for those looking for employment (geared toward the United Kingdom and Germany), a section for looking up company data for free, the Free Pint bar (a message board for asking those tough research questions), and a section on workshops related to information issues. Although these sections are useful for a specific purpose, the newsletter is the best tool for keeping current on the Web and search engines in general.

The Virtual Chase (http://www.virtualchase.com) is another fine resource to use for staying current with search engine technology, created and maintained by Genie Tyburski. There are two features of Virtual Chase: the research portal and TVC Alert. The research portal (found at http://www.virtualchase.com) provides users with a vast amount of information on using the Web as a research tool through articles, Internet research guides, and online teaching tools. Although Virtual Chase is mainly geared toward the legal profession, all librarians will benefit from the vast knowledge of research presented there.

TVC Alert, the corresponding free daily newsletter to Virtual Chase, is packed with news and web sites about the world of research. Here, Tyburski shows her knowledge of keeping current by always surprising the reader with new and valuable information and resources. She discusses search engines, legal databases, cases relevant to the information science profession, and always well-received practical advice. Readers will benefit by signing up for TVC Alert. Every morning, I can't wait for each new issue to arrive in my inbox.

News and press releases from the engines themselves can also be a valuable resource. Although the searcher must be wary of biased information obtained here (third parties such as the resources mentioned above are non-biased), many times the engines' news will be the most current. Every search engine company has either a press release or an "In the News" section (many have both), and they are usually archived back a few years. Most of the time, this information is found in the "About Us" section. For example, Altavista has a pressroom where releases are dated back to 1999. Articles about the company are also located there.

Search engines, like any other company out there, are looking to make money (remember, Google, Yahoo! and the others are not in it for the fun of providing search technology), so whenever they have the opportunity to toot their own horns about any aspect of their engine, they will do so. Note that they could also provide false information about their competition. To keep current, the searcher should look at news about engines from both the engines themselves and third parties.

OTHER RESOURCES WORTH NOTING

The sources mentioned above are a must to subscribe to and read if one wants to stay current with search engines. There are secondary sources that, every now and then, will provide new features that the others do not mention.

Search Engine Blog (http://www.searchengineblog.com) is a no-frills, quick listing of the daily events that pertain to engines. The Webmaster lets the articles speak for themselves. The posts are generally related to the field of search engine optimization but worth a swift glance, which will only take a few minutes.

Google Weblog (http://google.blogspace.com/) is dedicated to America's favorite search engine. This site always amazes me with its up-to-date news and web sites pertaining to Google. Sometimes the posts are informative, and at other times, hilarious. There is a posting either daily or every other day, and the postings are well worth reading. The author invites readers to send in any web sites or stories related to Google. Because this is such a wonderful tool, I wonder why other search engines do not have weblogs dedicated to them.

WHAT TO LOOK FOR IN SEARCH ENGINES

You now have seen the most useful resources for keeping current with the changing world of search engine technology. Certain aspects of these changes are of particular concern to any user of these engines. Because the content of every search engine changes on a daily basis (remember, search engines never search the "live" Web; they retrieve content from sites they have indexed at a certain point in time—sometimes weeks or even months prior), and the mathematical equations that affect the way results are displayed on these engines is somewhat secretive, tracking the options available to the user is of prime value. Listed here are the different ways that engines can change and why they are useful or not useful to the researcher.

Database Size

In all aspects of life, many people think "The bigger, the better." Just look at the SUV phenomenon that has swept the United States over the past decade. The same issue is prevalent in the search engine industry because the makers of the major search engines understand that if people believe that they are searching more web sites in a database, then they also believe that they will receive more relevant results and keep using that particular search engine. Although this is theoretically true, getting bogged down in numbers, especially when they get so large, seems fruitless.

The size of the engine database could matter if one performs such specific searches so as to retrieve fewer than ten results, but how many times has this happened? While performing research for my clientele, this will occasionally happen but not so much that I need to be concerned about database size. The key to using search engines is to know the basics (and beyond) of searching them, not their numeric magnitude. Don't get me wrong; size does matter if the numbers are smaller. I would rather search a database with two thousand documents than search a similar one with ten. I was once told that there is a vast difference between two people aged twenty-five and seventeen but not between two people aged eighty-five and seventy-seven. As the age increases, there is not much of a difference.

As of August 2002, only two of the major engines displayed the number of pages that were in their databases: Google counted 2,469,940,685, and Alltheweb displayed 2,112,188,990. These two have been battling for the top position for the past two years, with each one pulling ahead numerous times. Although we can only take educated guesses through results studies (http://www.searchengineshowdown.com/stats/size.shtml), the size of the engine should not matter to the user. There are more important aspects to worry about.

Fee-Based Results

Within the past few years, a trend has started that affects the results of almost every query performed on any search engine. Long considered the "purest" place in the Internet, where results were based only on special algorithmic equations, search engines have started to take payment for high placement of certain sites when specific keywords are used.

By bidding the highest on certain search terms, companies can get their web sites at the highest position on the search results page. These types of campaigns are flourishing as more and more Internet users use the power of search engines to find what they need. Overture (http://www.overture.com), the most prominent company behind these "paid placement" engines, provides the highest rankings to many of the major search engines, including Yahoo! Altavista, and Alltheweb.

"Paid inclusion," another relevant factor that may skew various search engine results, allows for Webmasters to pay for certain priorities on engines. In this scenario, the engine will reindex the web site more frequently (thus allowing the user to find more current information with a search) and allow for a deeper listing (thus providing the advertiser to be listed with a broad variety of search terms). Paid inclusion sites, unlike those for paid placement, do not appear in a separate section of the listings and could be scattered throughout the results.

Although these are not illegal practices (search engines, like any other company, need to make money to survive), librarians need to be aware that a top result for a particular keyword does not necessarily mean a better result. More important, information professionals need to advise their customers on these paid placement listings when assisting them with using engines. Along these lines, keeping current with paid placement and paid inclusion is essential to anyone using these engines on a daily basis.

The Federal Trade Commission has started to strongly recommend to search engine companies that they disclose which web sites in any given search results listing are paid placement or paid inclusion, so as not to confuse consumers (http://www.ftc.gov/os/closings/staff/commercialalertletter.htm). Although only in the early stages, these regulations will strongly enhance the user's ability to distinguish between the free and fee-based results.

Changes in Advanced Options

Advanced search options are probably the most underutilized, and most important, part of every search engine. These options, easily located on any search screen, allow the searcher to create a search strategy that will result in fewer hits from an engine. Most of these options are available within the main search bar, but the user would have to know the exact characters to use.

The advanced options allow the amateur web searcher to use these features without knowing the exact search string. For example, if I were using Google to search for the terms *waste* and *Michigan* but not *oil* and only non-profit domain names, I could put in the following search query: "waste Michigan -oil site:.org." I could do the same search without having to memorize each engine's advanced searching feature by using the impressive Google advanced options page. As this example shows, by using the advanced features, even the use of Boolean logic characters like AND or OR do not need to be memorized.

Examples of advanced search properties include simple requests, such as the use of phrases, and those that are more demanding, such as searching for sites in a particular language. Using the advanced search options may also reveal other parts of the search engine that are not visible from the front page, such as Google Uncle Sam (http://www.google.com/unclesam), a relatively older aspect of the engine that searches only government domains.

For librarians and other searchers to get the most out of the engines that they choose to use, continuous monitoring and knowledge of the advanced features will go a long way.

I received an Instant Message from a colleague not long ago. She had gotten a telephone call from her state library. They were performing a research query for one of their constituencies and were in need of a search engine that works with proximity operators (the ability to search for two words within a certain proximity from one another). Normally, I would have dismissed this as an unanswerable question as I had only seen this feature reserved for fee-based databases (e.g., Lexis Nexis or Westlaw).

However, after Google (http://www.google.com) released its API Developers Kit in 2001, proximity searching wasn't far behind. In short, API (Application Programming Interface) allows programmers to play with the syntaxes of the Google database to create their own search criteria (this will be discussed in more detail below). Soon after the API release, I was notified about GAPS (Google API Proximity Search) (http://www.staggernation. com/cgi-bin/gaps.cgi), a search interface that allows Google to be searched using the sought-after proximity operators. Although it only performs a search for words within one to three spots from one another, GAPS provides a piece of search technology where there previously was none.

API allows anyone (a username and password are free and mandatory) with programming knowledge to fiddle with the code and create his or her own search interface, complete with new and creative ways to use and search for content indexed by the Google engine.

The technology behind Google API goes well beyond the scope of this book, but the integration of the programming skills of thousands of computer experts with the massive database provides for a wondrous number of new tools. Two examples follow.

1. One useful Google API creation is the Google date search (http://www.faganfinder.com/engines/google.shtml), which allows the user to search the Google index by the date that information was indexed or reindexed (Google reindexes more than one million of its pages daily). This tool may be helpful if one is searching for new sites that have been added to the Google database.
2. Another neat tool that came out of Google API is a search by e-mail application (http://www.capescience.com/google/index.shtml). I am sometimes on the road and need to perform a quick Web search with no computer in site. Most phones have e-mail capabilities, and this tool allows the user to e-mail a query to Google, and results will be sent back within minutes.

The release of the Google API allows the searcher to have more control over the way the engine is searched. To find out about new resources that use this powerful tool, one should consult a listing from the Open Directory Project (http://directory.google.com/top/computers/internet/searching/search.engines/google/web.apis/) or the new book *Google Hacks* by Tara Calishain and Rael Domfest. As mentioned, Calishain is the creator of ResearchBuzz (http://www.researchbuzz.com) and the Buzz Toolbox (http: //www.buzztoolbox.com/google/), which has a list of Google API search mechanisms.[1]

In late 2002, Amazon.com joined the API fray by releasing its database to awaiting programmers. The tools that were developed assist the book searcher in many ways. Some examples follow.

Amazon Lite (http://www.kokogiak.com/amazon/) is for those who like to use Amazon.com but are bothered by the extra features, such as advertisements. Amazon Lite presents the results in a clean fashion, without all of the bells and whistles associated with the original site. The same content is there, just laid out differently. The catch? If you buy a book from this site (and it is safe and private), the Webmaster gets a cut of the proceeds via the Amazon Consumer Associates Program.

Book Watch (http://mockerybird.com/index.cgi?node=book+watch) displays the power of Amazon API, Google API, and a weblog tool called Book Watch (where books are gathered according to the number of mentions on weblogs) in a fun tool. This site provides a listing of books mentioned on Book Watch, with the book information gathered by Amazon API and related links using Google API.

Amazon RSS (http://www.yaywastaken.com/amazon/) is a site to keep in mind when reading chapter 5, about RSS and news aggregators. Without getting real technical here, this application sends the user new books listed in the Amazon database based on specific keywords of the user's choosing. This is a very powerful tool to find new releases on a certain subject.

The release of the Amazon database and Google APIs has been a smashing success throughout the web world. The fun and useful tools that have been created from these databases have enhanced and enriched the way searchers navigate these sometimes difficult and extensive applications. One would hope that other search engines and subject-specific databases enter the API fray.

NEW SEARCH ENGINES

While librarians keep abreast of changes in the engines that are currently in use by searchers around the globe, new engines continue to surface on a daily basis. Some of these engines are not worth a second look, but others need to be monitored for changes that may allow them to be on equal ground with the current leaders in the field. A quick evaluation of these new engines will enable the user to decide whether to continue to monitor them or toss them in the virtual recycling bin.

Although database size was not deemed important in the existing engines on the market, it should matter when dealing with newcomers, as size will dramatically affect the results of a search. The veteran engines have already established themselves as consistent players and do not need database size as a prerequisite for good search technology, but the new engines do. They have no history or previous experience to rely on, so database size should be a factor. Many new engines feel that they must compete with the Googles of the world and have started to present their size directly on their front page. For example, in the summer of 2002, a new engine entered the marketplace and immediately caught the eye of search engine researchers because of its size. Openfind (http://www.openfind.com), still in beta as of this writing, claimed to have more than 3.5 billion pages indexed in its database, about 500 million more than Google.

One of the many reasons Google has become a national phenomenon is ease of use. Also, most users like the relatively calm interface on the front page.

There are no lengthy banner ads, no news items, no shopping links—just a plain search bar, with the four tabs showing us the way to the other parts of Google, such as the extensive Usenet archive. If the new engine portrays a plain search interface, one may tend to like that particular tool, as it is easy on the eyes. One new engine that I have been watching for about a year is Gigablast (http://www.gigablast.com). Although the database size has fluctuated a lot over the year, the clean interface has impressed me.

Because search engines are not searching the "live" Web (only a snapshot of the Web taken on a particular day), it is imperative to know the last time a new engine has reindexed the data stored in the database. An old database does not help the researcher who is looking for current information. The user normally cannot tell the last time a site was indexed by the engine, although Google will provide this information for a few million of the sites in its index. In addition, the searcher may also be able to tell the last time a site was reindexed by utilizing the cache option in Google. Freshness should be a top priority for search engines and especially new engines that are looking to build up a client base and have repeat users.

Another important aspect of new engines is the searching capabilities. Does the engine have an advanced search feature? Is the Boolean logic explained in great detail? Librarians should be extra sensitive to these search capabilities as they have been trained in the use of database searching while in library school. The engines that have been successful over the years have offered an easy way to search by using AND as the default operator (the user does not have to use AND or + in the search query). At most, the engine should have an "About Us" or help section where all of the searching capabilities are explained. The searcher should be wary of any engine that does not take the time to help users search the database.

Out of every ten new engines that come on the scene during any given period, at least eight are meta-engines (that search multiple databases at once and not a unique one). Although meta-engines are popular among web users, one should be wary of the claims that they make. Many "metas" relay false information as to the databases that are included in their sites. For example, I was fond of an engine called Metor (http://www.metor.com) because it apparently searched many of my favorite databases including Google, Alltheweb, and Altavista. While I thought that Metor was serving up results from Google, it was not. As librarians are well aware, false information provides no confidence in a resource. Also, many meta-engines have only a selection of results from engines that they claim are part of their search engine collection. My advice: test this by performing the exact same search on both the meta-engine and the one that it claims to carry. In addition, because search engines incorporate different Boolean logic schema and algorithmic equations to provide results, meta-engines have difficulty providing relevant hits from all engines, as they use the same search schema for each one.

It is also important to use the same search queries when testing engines. First, the results will be familiar. The searcher will be able to tell right away whether the engine is providing the highest-level results and if they are current. A variety of terms is also recommended, as the engine will display its knack for issues such as quotes around phrases, Boolean logic, and default properties. Once these terms are established, it would behoove the user to continuously use these terms to test the same engines, as the standards may change without notice from the engine. Using the same terms will immediately point out these changes as the user is used to the results.

THE GOOGLE "PROBLEM"

Although Google is clearly the search engine of choice of most librarians and web users, I believe there is a "Google problem" prevalent. Although Google is one of the best engines to search the Web (there is no denying that), I worry that some are becoming too dependent on it. They automatically assume that Google will find the answers to their questions.

For example, one day in my office, I was approached by a customer who asked if I knew of any books that would help with the necessary steps to incorporate a business in New York and a discussion about any issues that may arise. I immediately thought of a treatise that the library had recently purchased that would be perfect. Another attorney overheard us and told the attorney, "You don't need that book; just go to Google.com, type in 'New York incorporation and Secretary of State,' and the answer will be right there. You don't need a book for that."

I retrieved the book from the library stacks and brought it out to the first attorney and showed him the section on incorporating a business in New York. I mentioned that, yes, Google is one of the best search engines out there, but it is not the "be all and end all" of the Web. I threw out statistics (Google only indexes less than one-quarter of the entire Web, other engines have web sites that Google doesn't, etc.) and discussed in detail the problem of the Invisible Web. My patrons immediately knew that this was not the first time I had dealt with "homage" to Google.

Although Google will be able to find answers to many queries, I worry what happens when it doesn't. As this engine becomes more of the norm, many will be led to believe that if they did not find it on Google, then it doesn't exist on the Web. This is completely wrong, and librarians and information professionals need to continue to explain this to their customers. Keeping current with search technology not only brings other engines into play, but almost forces the user to remember that these other valid (and sometimes better than Google) engines exist.

NEWS ENGINES

One of the easiest ways to catch up with the news is by using the many news-specific engines that are currently on the market. These engines index thousands of news sources on a frequent basis (most of the time every hour or less) and provide users with relevant, up-to-date information on any search query. Although they do not index as many resources as a fee-based database would, news search engines are a viable tool for the information professional. Some users search for current news items using the general search engines. Although some engines provide news within the results of their searches, the information may be a few days, weeks, or even months old. I have even seen news stories from three years prior to the day that I was searching. This may be fine for historical research, but it is not useful for the librarian looking to stay current.

Five news-specific engines will be discussed in this section: two come from major portals (Yahoo! and Google), and three are stand-alone news engines.

Yahoo! has always been known for its breaking-news service, categorizing current news into subfolders in its breaking-news section. Besides this service, there is also a search engine (http://news.yahoo.com) attached where users can search for relevant news. Over the years, Yahoo! has forged relationships with the major wires (Associated Press, Business Wire, Reuters) to bring their users late-breaking news items. These wires are indexed into the Yahoo! News search database. There are many advanced options in the news database plus an alert listing that will send updated news via e-mail. This engine does not index as many resources as the others mentioned below, but it is still a viable resource to use for keeping current.

Google News (http://news.google.com), the beta version of Google's news engine, was released in March 2002. The entire engine is created on the fly, with no manual entering of data. Keeping with the Google tradition, the articles whose subjects are most written about in their database will appear on top. The main interface has the most popular news, categorized into general subjects, with the query engine on top. As of March 2003, Google had indexed news from more than four thousand sources. After a search is performed, the engine brings back a results list that looks similar to the main engine result, with the keyword in boldface. Google News can display the results sorted by date or relevance. For users who are trying to find out what is happening in their fields, the relevancy aspect is helpful, but for those who are constantly keeping track of their profession on a continuous basis throughout the day, the date function is the one to choose. Most of the Boolean and advanced capabilities available on the general engine are available in Google News as well. What sets this engine apart from most is the ability to index local newspapers in addition to the national news.

Moreover (http://www.moreover.com) is another engine whose only mission is to index and serve up news to the user. Its main focus is on providing breaking news that the Webmasters can place on web sites or newsletters. For example, Search Day, the search engine newsletter mentioned above, provides the latest news about search engines directly from the Moreover index. This database also provides e-mail alerts for subject-specific topics (http://www.moreover.com/cgi-local/page?o=portal). There are more than one hundred topics for the user to choose from. These e-mail alerts are sent out daily with news on the subjects that the user has chosen. Moreover was one of the first news engines on the market and has continued to grow into a vast resource for news junkies. *See also* chapter 5, on RSS feeds, to learn how to incorporate any Moreover search into a news aggregator.

World News (http://www.wn.com) is another news search engine that indexes many popular news web sites and some underutilized databases. World News is set apart from the others by its ability to scan news from non-American resources that publish in English. The main interface is covered with resources for the user to take advantage of, such as the numerous international news sites. The search query is basic, with the only option being how many results are displayed on the page (I usually choose one hundred). The first fifty words of the news item are displayed along with the title of the article. I have been using World News for four years and have found that it indexes articles that are not found in any other engine.

Finally, **Rocket News** (http://www.rocketnews.com/search/index.html) provides the user with another resource for searching news. Like World News, there are no bells or whistles in Rocket News, but there is a simple advanced engine where the user can limit the search using Boolean operators. The search can also be limited to the number of days searched (between one and five from which to pull news). The search results provide the title of the article and the first twenty-five words.

Specialized news engines are useful in that their only focus is on the news; thus, they work constantly to build up their databases. Using a few of these engines while searching for the day's news should provide an overall view of what is happening for a particular keyword. For the librarian attempting to keep current, placing the term *library* or *librarian* into one or more of these engines will pull up many articles worth reading.

Search engines will continue to be used on a daily basis by librarians and their patrons. In fact, a recent study published by the Pew Internet and American Life Project mentioned that search engines are the most frequently used method for finding information on the Web (http://www.pewinter net.org/reports/toc.asp?report=80). This may not come as a shock to professional Web searchers, but it is of extreme importance that new search engine users use these search methods properly and to their utmost capabilities. It is also the job of the librarian to keep up with the changes to these engines and to pass this information on to the customers.

With the sources and methods mentioned above, librarians should be able to stay abreast of the changes to the major search engines.

NOTE

1. Tara Calishain and Rael Domfest, *Google Hacks* (Sebastopol, Calif.: O'Reilly, 2003).

3 Web Site Monitoring Software

I love getting e-mail newsletters. In fact, signing up for them is the easiest way to keep current with the content on a particular site. Just enter your e-mail address (and sometimes a password), and you will be notified of any changes in the site via a monthly, weekly, or, even better, daily newsletter. There are no programs to open, no software to download. It's that easy. Unfortunately, only a few web sites that I frequent have this capability.

Keeping current is about speed and how quickly the user can inhale all of the relevant content from multiple sources, filter out the irrelevant noise, organize the information for later retrieval, and still have time to perform the regular daily activities. Because e-mail is the one standard tool, retrieving new content via this medium every day should theoretically be the quickest avenue.

But the question remains: how can one quickly keep current using e-mail for sites that do not offer newsletters for notification of new material added to their site? Enter web site monitoring software and the web-tracking services it provides.

Put simply, using web site monitoring software, web-tracking services will monitor any sites that users have specified and notify them when any changes have occurred on that particular page. Web users do not have to return to each page every morning to see if any changes have occurred. The software will do it for them. Usually, these web-tracking software products require little setup. For the "nontechie" like me, this is a necessity. If I am not able to completely run any tool in about fifteen minutes, it is not worth my precious time.

The theme of this book is building up resources and search techniques to help in answering reference questions and for professional development purposes. These tracking services are a perfect companion for both of these purposes. First, for reference queries, by receiving new content from a favorite list of links, librarians will be able to add to their repertoire numerous resources. This, in turn, should enable the reference staff to answer questions quickly and more efficiently. Second, using these web-tracking services, librarians can quickly read about current events in the field of library and information science without having to spend time visiting multiple web sites. They can spend more time helping to meet the information needs of patrons.

Over the past few years, these web-tracking services have become more complex, with more features added every time these tools are upgraded. Thus, evaluating them has become more difficult. Finding the device that completely suits the needs of the user is a rare occasion in any field, and web site monitoring software is no exception. This chapter aims to display the many features of web site monitoring software, describe how to evaluate them, and review many of the key players in this field.

FEATURES AND EVALUATIONS

Like many other things on the Web, some web-tracking services cost money. Others do not cost anything, while still others will track a certain number of sites for free, with the opportunity to track more for a fee. Although I always advocate for free web content and software, users should compare the services offered by each company to decide whether the free tool is better for their needs. The costs may outweigh these needs or the cost of the tool might not be a factor, considering the time saved by using these tools. Most of the web-tracking tools do not exceed $50 for an annual or onetime fee, and this low price may not be a consideration. Consider the other options before deciding on the free tool just because you don't have to take out your credit card. In other words, try to get the most "bang for your buck."

Another factor to look for is the way the new content is delivered. Some devices will deliver the full content of all sites via one long e-mail, while others will send each individual site in separate e-mails. In addition, sometimes the company will only send a link that the user has to click on to get to the information. Note whether the software allows for e-mail delivery or if you have to go to the site and log in to retrieve the new content.

Another issue to keep in mind when deciding which service to use is the software itself. Does it need to be downloaded or is it web based? If it can be accessed via the Web, chances are that it can be used from any computer with Internet access. This is important for librarians who have to share a computer with colleagues or who are not allowed to download software at work.

How easy is it to add new web pages? Obviously, if the tracking devices are web based, one would need to log in, but once that is done, are other steps needed to add sites that the user wants to track? Sometimes the makers of the software provide a JavaScript button that the user places in the links section of the browser. When a web page is found that the user wants to monitor, it can be added to the account by the click of that button. Because time is a key factor in keeping current, time should also be considered when using these tools. How long it takes to perform other tasks should be noted as well. Finally, many of these products will provide a button that can be placed on web sites so that visitors can easily add the URL to the tracking software.

For tools that send e-mail with a link back to the software that contains the changes, are the changes easy to see? Sometimes the user will only be notified when a certain page has changed, but the new content is not high-lighted, and one must search for it. Software that provides links and highlights new content provides a quick way to scan the site for new information. Also, if the notification is sent via e-mail, does it have all of the changes that occurred on a particular page or only a certain number of keywords? Not only is time important, but the accuracy of the tool is a contributing factor as well.

Once you are acquainted with one particular tool, and many sites have been inserted for monitoring, it may start to get unruly. I monitor more than 250 sites, and I sometimes spend a good twenty minutes looking for relevant material because of the high amount of content. To reduce the time, some monitoring tools allow for keyword limitations that will only provide new content if it includes or doesn't include certain keywords. Although this feature definitely reduces the number of results that are provided, the odds of missing an important news item or web site are greater. Thus, be careful how these keywords are used.

In the search engine world, the better the advanced options, the more relevant the results will be. With monitoring services, the more options available to the user, the more satisfied the user will be with the product. When evaluating web-tracking services, be especially attentive of these options as they could make or break a decision to use a particular product. Compare options between two products. What does one have that the other doesn't? How important are certain options to the user? Which ones can't you live without and which ones are not so important?

At times, especially on the weekends, a day or two will go by where one hasn't had a chance to check the software. Maybe life at the reference desk was too busy, or a much-needed vacation was necessary. If this happens, will all of the content from the previous few days be available or will it disappear and leave only the new material from the current day? If the full text of the new material is sent via e-mail, then it will be stored in your inbox, but if links to the site are provided, the new content may be gone. This may be a blessing in disguise, however, as it may take a while to catch up.

Finally, if the user runs into trouble, how does the site assist in answering any questions? Is the FAQ readily available, and is it well stocked with helpful information? Is there an FAQ? Does the company provide contact information for e-mail questions and concerns? If so, does the company get back to you in a reasonably quick fashion and with a valid answer?

Consider all of these factors before investing time (and, more important, money) in any of the following web site monitoring products.

WEB SITE MONITORING RESOURCES

Watch That Page (WTP) (http://www.watchthatpage.com) is a free service that will track an infinite number of web sites of the user's choosing. This service will track changes in web sites and deliver the results to the user via e-mail, or, if the user prefers, he or she can log on to the web site and look at the changes. WTP does not require any software to be downloaded; thus, the user can gain access to any account via any computer with Internet access. There are two ways to add a new web site for tracking. The user can log in to the account, click on the "pages" tab, and enter the URL. Second, the site provides a JavaScript bookmarklet (a tool that extends the browse capabilities in the browser) that can be added to the links section of many popular browsers (Internet Explorer, Netscape, and Opera currently support this feature). If one finds a site that is deemed "trackable," the site can be automatically added to the sites being viewed by clicking on the bookmarklet. This saves precious time.

WTP will only provide new content from sites to the user. The information need not be highlighted as the service only displays the new text of the tracked web site, not a link to the site itself, like many of the other services that will be discussed. Not only will the new content be shown, but all new links on each site are displayed as well. The time it takes to read the new content is cut down tremendously because of the reduction of steps.

WTP also provides for keyword searching, which will also cut down on the number of results. The user can choose multiple words in an OR or AND format or even restrict the results by using a phrase. Although keyword searching is highly recommended for those who intend to track many web sites, those who want a complete display of new content on a particular subject may choose not to use this option, as it is possible that it will miss a valid resource.

The advanced search features (*see* figure 3-1) for WTP are not as grandiose as one would hope but are worth mentioning. First, the user can choose the times that the e-mail is sent. For example, I check my e-mail at home twice a day, once in the morning and once in the evening. Thus, I get two notifications per day from WTP. This is especially useful as I monitor numerous sites, too many to review in one sitting. Also, one can set the option to only receive one e-mail per week (the user decides which day), but again, this is not recommended for those who monitor a lot of sites as well as for those looking to remain current on a daily basis. There is also an option to receive a listing of only the pages that have changed, but I have yet to find any use

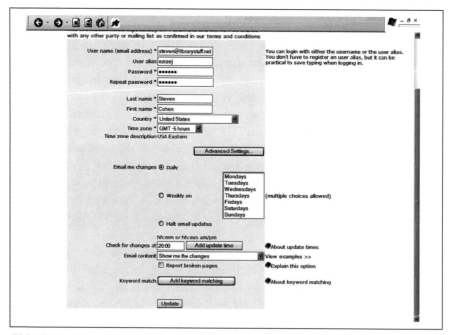

FIGURE 3-1   Watch That Page—Configuration

for this, unless one is only monitoring the change in the site, not the actual content. Finally, like electronic discussion lists, one has the option to temporarily cease this service for a vacation or other activities that would create a backlog of e-mail messages.

The options prevalent in the "Your Pages" section are worth documenting as well. Each monitored site can be placed into hierarchical folders for storage purposes, making it easy to review the source, verify that the page is being monitored, or delete the site. The pages can also be switched easily from one folder to the next. The prevalence of these folders eases the burden of finding the monitored pages, but WTP will only display each site in alphabetical order (*see* figure 3-2). If the daily or weekly e-mail were listed in a hierarchical manner, in relation to the folders it occupies, the reading of the content would perhaps move more quickly. Plus, if one is monitoring sites for two separate jobs, reading all the new content for each job consecutively would provide for easier transition between assignments.

One last note about WTP. The new content from each page is saved on WTP's server for a lengthy period of time. I have been able to retrieve

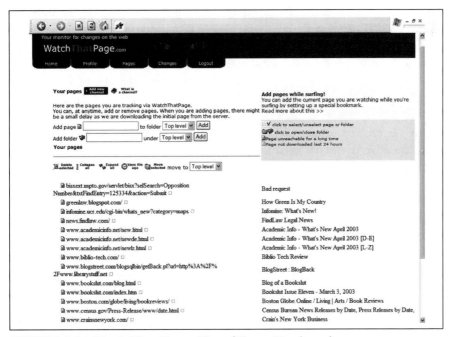

FIGURE 3-2   Watch That Page—List of Pages Monitored

content from at least two weeks prior. This is a wonderful feature for those who will be away from a computer for a given amount of time but would like to continuously monitor web sites. Also, because the new content is sent via e-mail, only these mailings need to be saved to catch up after being away.

As mentioned above, WTP is free. Although users may suspect and question any online company that provides a free service similar to others that charge a fee (especially during this time of the digital demise), I have one suggestion. Take advantage of it while you can.

Infominder (http://www.infominder.com) is another web-based web site tracking tool that allows for free monitoring of up to ten sites. To track the content from more than the ten sites, a $25 fee is required (then up to one hundred sites may be monitored). Infominder does not require software to be downloaded; thus, it can be accessed from any computer.

Infominder is different from WTP in that it will provide the new content as a link to a cached version of the page that resides on the Infominder server. All of the links are live, which will allow the user to continue working directly from this cached page. The new content is highlighted so the user can easily pick it out without having to reread old information. Every day, this service will e-mail the user a link to this cached page as well as some of the text of the new content. Thus, to get the complete changes, visitors must go to the cached pages with highlights. There is an additional step to be taken here, compared to WTP, which may play into the amount of time the user has to review new content. Infominder also allows users to add RSS (Rich Site Summary or Really Simple Syndication) feeds to the pages being monitored. Briefly, RSS feeds are a form of XML (Extensible Markup Language) used for headline syndication (RSS will be discussed at length in chapter 5). One of the reasons for using RSS is to glean only the content of the site rather than the advertisements or other useless features always prevalent on commercial sites.

Adding URLs to Infominder is a bit more tedious than WTP. Although there is not a bookmarklet available, Infominder does offer a tool that allows for easy transition of proposed sites to monitor into the system. Users need to download a small attachment, "IE Assistant"; once installed, it will allow users to add a site by right clicking on the mouse. This feature is available for Microsoft Internet Explorer and Netscape browsers only, and it isn't as easy as a bookmarklet (because it needs to be downloaded), but it can be useful when one wants to add sites to be tracked as soon as they are found rather than having to remember to log on and add them manually. However, because Infominder only allows one to track ten sites for free, if one chooses not to purchase the upgraded version, it doesn't seem worthwhile to bother down-loading "IE Assistant."

Infominder does allow for keyword searching of the results from the various tracked sites. Users can choose as many keywords as needed and use them in an OR or AND fashion. Thus, either all or any of the words need to be present. Again, this feature would only seem to be worthwhile for track-ing a multitude of web sites.

The advanced search features for Infominder are vast and very useful (*see* figure 3-3). First, one can place each of the tracked sites into hierarchical cat-egories and provide a description for each page. Also, Infominder will allow for sites that require an ID and password to be tracked. Users just need to provide the proper identification. For aesthetic purposes, one can also choose the colors of the highlighted content in the monitored URLs. In addition, users can provide different e-mail addresses for each monitor. This is especially useful for those who track sites for different reasons, such as for work and per-sonal situations, and use separate e-mail addresses. Finally, one can also choose the frequency of the updates.

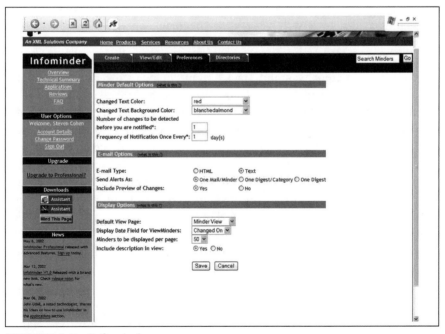

FIGURE 3-3   Infominder

Because the pages are cached on the Infominder server, only one day of new content is saved for the user. Even if one saves the daily e-mail alerts, the content from that URL will only be from the current date. Thus, this tool may not be useful for those who do not check their e-mail at least once per day.

Finally, the free version of Infominder provides updates only once per day, which may be enough for the average user. For those who have the time for more than one update per day, the fee-based version will provide updates every half hour or more.

Track Engine (http://www.trackengine.com) is similar to Infominder in that there is a limited number of free sites to track (five as compared to ten) and many options available to the user. Two features are available to those who upgrade to the fee-based version. First, for $4.95 per month, one can receive up to fifty additional bookmarks to track. Second, the sites that are to be tracked will be monitored more often (up to every hour, if desired). The two features mentioned here are the most common for upgrades, as the companies would not make any money by giving away the product for free. As mentioned in chapter 2, these companies need to make money to survive.

Track Engine will send new content via e-mail in four formats. One can choose to receive the new content as a web page with the new content highlighted, as a link to a web page with the new content highlighted, in a summary with the web page without any highlights, and in a summary with a link to the page without highlights. Each page that is monitored can be done so in a different way, and Track Engine helps in the decision-making process by providing advice to suit the users' needs. Track Engine is one of the few sites that will send the entire page in html format via e-mail with the changes highlighted, which can cut down on the amount of time to access new content. However, this causes a greater amount of space to be taken up in the e-mail software, which can be a problem for those with limited space.

Narrowing down the number of results via keyword is also available with this web tool, and the system is more advanced than those previously mentioned. For example, Track Engine allows for limitations by phrases. For example, if one wants to receive updates for pages that only have the phrase *computer equipment* or *trademark infringement,* this can be accomplished for each bookmark separately. Although this feature can be very useful, it may narrow down the results too much, in that the user may not receive any new content and may miss important information that appears in a slightly different format. Wildcards are also available, which means that any word(s) can appear within a phrase, for example, "librarians * books." Again, though a noble effort on behalf of the Webmasters at Track Engine, this may only provide a small number of results and may cause other important updates to be overlooked. As with the other engines, the keyword-matching feature uses Boolean operators to narrow down results.

Like WTP, there are two ways to add desired pages to be tracked in Track Engine. First, because there is no software to download, one can add pages from any computer with Internet access. Just log in and add the URL. A bookmarklet is also available. Simply drag the "Watch Me" link to the toolbar on the browser, and click it when a desired page is accessed to quickly add it to Track Engine.

There are numerous advanced options available on Track Engine, far too many to discuss here, but there are a few worth mentioning that do not appear on those tools discussed previously. First, this tool stands alone in offering the reports via a Personal Digital Assistant (PDA), which allows for a more portable usage of tracking software. Actually, I am surprised that more tracking companies don't offer this service, as the whole point is to keep current in a quick fashion. It would only make sense that this could be accomplished whenever the user wants. Second, Track Engine allows the option of monitoring changes in hyperlinks, images, numbers, and dates. The other tracking software will display changes in unimportant aspects of the page, such as the change in dates, but Track Engine will only do so if selected by the user.

Just as Al Gore accused George W. Bush of using "fuzzy math" to win the presidential election in 2000, Track Engine users have the option of utilizing a "fuzzy matching" technique to avoid unnecessary changes in the content of web sites. By clicking on this option in the settings folder, very minor changes in sentences or paragraphs will not be flagged as new. This option allows for only drastic changes in pages to be displayed. As discussed previously, options such as these will help in narrowing down the content, but there is more likelihood that important information might be missed. To be sure, it is a give-and-take situation.

Web Site Watcher (WSW) (http://aignes.com/) is different from the previously mentioned monitoring software in that it needs to be downloaded to a computer. This tool may not be appropriate for those who use more than one computer and would like to track changes throughout the day. WSW also does not allow for any pages to be tracked for free. The software can be downloaded on a trial basis for thirty days, and it costs $29.95, with free upgrades.

The software interface has a Microsoft Outlook look to it, divided into three sections, with numerous options on top. A list of folders is situated on the left side, the sites that are being watched are on the top right portion, and an internal browser is on the bottom right. Clicking on the option button in the software and entering the URL can easily add web sites. Also, if the software is continuously running on the desktop, the web browser will be equipped with a button that allows sites to be added to WSW on the fly.

WSW will notify the user of any changes to the desired web sites in a small pop-up screen. The new content can easily be checked by looking in the folder marked "Changed Bookmarks." The web page will then be opened with the new content highlighted. The changed content can also be e-mailed to the user, a feature that I always recommend using, as most information professionals use e-mail as a communication tool because of the convenience. The options for e-mail include sending the new content or the new page or an html version of the page with the changes highlighted. In the case of WSW, it is also easy to launch the program and check out the changes as well, a plus when using downloaded software.

Keyword searching is also available for WSW. Similar to Track Engine, WSW enables specific keyword searching for each site being tracked, a wonderful option if the content of tracked sites is different. For example, if I were to track the site for the American Library Association, I may use the following keywords: *banned, copyright,* or *read.* I wouldn't use the same keywords if I wanted to monitor the site for new books that appear in Amazon.com (unless, of course, I was interested in books on banning, copyright, or reading). The point is that it is logical to use keywords specific to the site being monitored. Also, WSW will allow different keywords to be highlighted in different colors, an option not available in any other web site monitoring tools.

If one looks for advanced features in deciding on a product, look no further than WSW. The options are too multitudinous to go into detail in this book, but a few features will be mentioned. First, one can easily set up the software to automatically check the sites for changes as often as every minute. Entitled "Autowatch," a clock will run backward from the desired time, review each site when the time expires, and notify the user of any changes. I imagine this tool as being useful for those in the corporate arena where a customer wants information the minute that it happens. I have been personally on the receiving end of such a request. Second, any errors in accessing a site will be placed in a folder marked *error,* which will immediately be seen by the user and, one hopes, rectified. Third, if one has collected a lengthy list of bookmarks over the years, WSW can easily add these sites to the software, saving the precious time of entering them in manually. Finally, one can jot down electronic notes within each site if time is short or for use later.

Because the changed sites can be e-mailed to the user, the new content can be kept for as many days as needed. Also, the new content can be saved to the hard drive and accessed offline, so there is no limit to the amount of days that the information can be saved.

In addition, because WSW is downloaded software, one can easily avoid retrieving any new changes in content by not launching the program. WSW will run only when you want it to run, which can be detrimental for those who still would like to receive changes while on vacation for use upon return. To have WSW run while on an extended trip, the computer would have to be left on, with WSW continuously running. Web content sometimes disappears as quickly as it appears, and this new information will be missed if WSW is not used for an extended period of time.

Like the other web content monitoring tools, WSW is very user-friendly, with an extensive help section. As mentioned previously, the point of using these tracking tools is to save the time and aggravation of having to manually visit sites to monitor changes. A tool that is difficult to use will not bode well for the researcher who has to take an inordinate amount of time trying to figure out how it works. Ease of use is important.

Many other tools can be used to track changes in web pages. The following tools deserve mention.

Tracerlock (http://www.tracerlock.com) is a web-based tool that monitors changes in news sites that have been chosen by the company and allows the customer to create personalized searches for any URL. Keyword searching is also available. Tracerlock is a bit more expensive than the previous tools, but the system works a bit differently. For $4 per month (Tracerlock is available for a thirty-day trial), this tool will run one keyword once a day in numerous news sites with the results of the new content e-mailed to the user. This tool does not show the news sites that are available for searching, which would be a necessity for me if I were to pay $4 per month for each keyword.

Change Detection (http://www.changedetection.com/) is a no-nonsense, no-frills service that allows users to monitor sites for changes at no cost. Just plug in the URL and your e-mail address, and you will be notified if that site changes. Only a link to the URL is sent, and the new content is not highlighted. This tool is useful for those who want a quick but not advanced way of monitoring pages for changes.

Web2mail (http://www.web2mail.com) is a free service that will send the html version (not text only) of web site pages to a specified e-mail address once a day regardless of whether changes have been made to those pages (the user can decide the time it is to be sent). There is no limit on the number of sites to be mailed, and the pages can be organized in hierarchical subject categories. Plus, a free e-mail account is available.

Botbox (http://www.botbox.com) is software that is downloaded and comes with many news items from Moreover (http://www.moreover.com) and other sources preinstalled. If these aren't enough, the user can then add other sites to be monitored. The list of new materials is displayed in a newspaper format (all of the links are displayed on one page), which has the advantage of the user not having to return to the main screen to look at new material from other sources. Botbox does not have the numerous advanced features that are available from the other software, but it may be worth checking out when comparing tools.

POTENTIAL USES FOR WEB SITE MONITORING TOOLS

Now that the many web site monitoring tools have been reviewed at length and the pros and cons revealed, we turn our attention to the type of information that could be monitored. This list is not extensive, as, theoretically, any site can be monitored for changes. However, here are a few suggestions that may not have been thought of at first glance.

Every company or organization will provide press releases on their respective web sites. Up-to-date information on these companies can usually come in the form of these news releases directly from the company. Although biased (no company would release deleterious information unless forced to), press releases are sometimes the first place that big news from companies is found. For example, at the end of 2002, Yahoo! announced that it was taking over another search engine company, Inktomi. The first accounts of this acquisition came from the press release section from each company's web site. When the news media read this, they pounced all over the story, and by the next day, everyone was reading about it.

Gathering information about companies from press releases alone can be detrimental to the research being performed. As mentioned above, these releases tend to be one-sided and shouldn't be the only resource used to gather data. Part of my job is to gather data on companies, and when they have a web site from which to glean information, I always tell the attorney for whom I am performing the task where I found the information.

Web site monitoring tools are best used for data that appear within an already existing set of information, such as lengthy links pages. Because the monitoring software highlights or e-mails the new material to the user, it is then brought to the forefront. An example of this type of resource is Academic Info (http://www.academicinfo.net), a web directory of web sites usually pertaining to the academic community but useful for all users. Academic Info has a portion of the site, which displays the new sites that have been added to the directory throughout the month (http://www. academicinfo.net/new.html). These new sites are placed in a subject hierarchy, not in chronological order, and it would be almost impossible to find new sites that are added daily. With the various web site monitoring software, the news sites that have been added will be highlighted or e-mailed. The user need not remember what the site looked like the last time it was viewed to determine the new material.

News search engines are a popular tool used by librarians in reference work to find current information on any topic. If one wanted to continue monitoring a particular search that was performed on one of the various news engines, then web site monitoring tools will come in handy. After querying the engine, place the URL that appears in the address bar (it will most likely be a lengthy address) into the monitoring tool, and every time a new news story appears, it will be highlighted or e-mailed. For example, I track news on the terms *librarian, library,* and *libraries* for professional development reasons on five of the major news engines: Google (http://news.google.com), Rocketinfo (http://www.rocketinfo.com), World News (http://www.wn.com), Moreover (http://www.moreover.com), and Yahoo! News (http://news.yahoo.com). When I log on to my monitoring tool, I am shown all of the new articles in which those words appear. Special librarians can use this feature to track businesses as well, sometimes finding out important information about a company before the company itself knows.

Online magazines that publish articles once a month are perfect for monitoring software mechanisms. At times, these sites will have an e-mail newsletter that goes out every time new monthly articles have been published, but if this feature is not available, one would not forget to return to the site at the beginning of every month. One of the most useful features of web site monitoring software is that once a site is found that warrants tracking, the user could literally forget that the site was visited. The monitoring tools have the memory necessary to perform this task.

When performing a very narrow search on any search engine, consider tracking that search in web site monitoring software, as any new entries indexed by those engines may prove useful in the future. This is yet another way to track a company, maybe to ascertain if any other company has mentioned it on its web site. Also, it is possible that someone has damaged the reputation of a business and has posted such damaging statements on a personal web site. Tracking search queries is also a method for finding trademark or intellectual property breaches by easily locating sites that illegally use a company's registered trademark.

Monitoring search queries is also a great way to find new sites on a particular subject. That said, a general search usually brings up a very large number of results. Although web site monitoring software is designed to pick up only the new material, it will often highlight material already appearing in the index. This may happen for a variety of reasons. First, the pages are often reindexed by the engine, and the summary that appears underneath the link changes with the reindexing; thus, the monitoring software is usually not able to distinguish the old from the new, even with the extensive filtering technology built into the programs. Second, because the results may overflow into multiple pages, it is likely that the results will appear on different pages and thus be seen as new by the software. One way to attempt control over this latter situation is to set the options on the engine to display the maximum number of hits per page. For example, Google can display one hundred results on one search result page.

Another way to continuously track specific subject-oriented web sites is by utilizing the subfolders inherent in web directories, such as Yahoo! (http://www.yahoo.com), the Open Directory Project (http://dmoz.org), or the Librarians' Index to the Internet (http://www.lii.org). These sites became famous for their extensive links and categorization schema. The odds of missing an important site are slim if one monitors the respective folders in each directory. The one issue that may arise here would be if a new site were placed in a different folder. Users of web-tracking software who do not place limits on the number of sites that can be monitored should try to be as liberal as possible when tracking folders for new entries.

Weblogs are discussed at length in chapter 4, but they are worth mentioning here as a perfect example of their use in tracking programs. Weblogs are constantly updated with new content on a daily, sometimes hourly basis. For those who want to be constantly updated with material that is published on any weblog, tracking software is a great option because one can set them up to check for updates at any time. Chapter 5 demonstrates that many users follow weblogs using RSS feeds, but for those who do not have this option, tracking software is a key device for reading new content on weblogs.

The federal and state governments are well known for the plethora of information that they release through their numerous agencies. On each of the various agencies' sites, there is usually a section on new additions, which could include newly released reports, new programs that the agency has created, and other important new features to the site. In the field of library and information science, one might monitor the site for the Institute of Museum and Library Services (http://www.imls.gov). For up-to-date information dealing with environmental issues, the EPA is an option (http://www.epa.gov). There are many sections to these bureaucratic web sites, and one may need to dig around to find the relevant information.

Finally, and maybe the most important, is the monitoring of the monitoring software itself. It would behoove the user to have the most up-to-date version of the software or, if the system is web based, to know about any new features that may be released. It also may be beneficial to monitor the competition, as certain changes may enforce a change in products.

PROBLEMS WITH TRACKING SOFTWARE

Despite a surge in the use of web site monitoring software, they do have drawbacks. As with all of the tools for currency mentioned in this book, it is possible that knowledge and use may become a cause of, rather than a tool to avoid, information overload. It is very easy to sign up for or download these services at a small cost and add sites to be monitored. Because of this, too many services may be monitored, and users may take too much of their time perusing sites that are of no help in keeping current or for use in reference work. Although I have always advocated for ease of use when it comes to any type of software, it is also important to use restraint when using software so as not to get carried away. Those who keep current must constantly focus on the tasks at hand and develop the skills necessary to avoid preoccupation with the usual Internet browsing distractions.

Because time is always a factor when dealing with currency (librarians should strive to gain access to the most pertinent information in the least amount of time), setting up and maintaining any web-tracking device can become burdensome. For example, when using WSW, there is an option to weed out the web site data that continuously change on a daily basis, such as the date and time, and the coding for taking out this information is different depending on how the date is shown. For example, if the date is displayed as 12-5-2003, a different set of commands is necessary than if the date is displayed as December 5, 2003. If one is monitoring more than two hundred sites and does not want time wasted because of false updates, then these options must be maintained, and this takes time. That said, it is well worth spending the time in the beginning when adding sites to the monitoring software, as time will be saved in the long run. Some users may be intimidated or confused by the useless content that finds its way into the web site monitoring software (like the date scenario mentioned above), but working with the software to make sure that only new content is displayed is well worth the time. This is where RSS feeds, discussed in chapter 5, become so useful, as only the content is brought to the forefront.

Another factor that none of these programs addresses is the issue of disappearing pages. These programs and web-based media only show the user the new material that appears on various web sites and tend to neglect the data that are removed. Sometimes features in search engines are not available anymore or an advanced search function is missing in a favorite online database. Information that disappears is sometimes more important than the new additions, as it may show a trend in what the web site is planning on doing with further material. In a world where our state and federal governments have been deleting information from their web sites, a tool that would discover that which is disappearing would benefit the library community greatly.

Web site monitoring tools are useful, timesaving avenues to choose for gaining access to new material on any web page. There are some factors to consider when deciding which tool to use. They include the limit, or lack thereof, of the number of sites that can be monitored; the price of the software; the downloaded or web-based log-in factor; its ease of use; the availability of folders to manage the web pages being monitored; and the availability of tech support. Once users become acquainted with this form of technology, fondness usually ensues because of the time that can be saved, not only in keeping abreast of news and new material in information science, but in every aspect of their lives online.

Weblogs 4

One of the obvious benefits of the Web is its potential for users to add their views on the world to its vast enterprise. Web pages are relatively easy to set up, and by using WYSIWYG (What You See Is What You Get) software, such as Microsoft Frontpage, web site owners need not know any code to establish an online presence. In addition, the cost of running a web site is cheap. Actually, one needs not invest a dime in creating a web site, in that a small space can be reserved for the price of having an advertisement displayed (e.g., Geocities) or time can be invested in learning html (the general coding scheme behind a basic web page) or a colleague might help with the web design. As the tools for creating web pages became easier to use over the years, it is no accident that another method has surfaced that makes this process even easier while in the meantime creating an outlet for aspiring writers, professionals, and others to publish their material online.

Enter the weblog (or blog, for short). Weblogs are a chronological listing of postings to a web site with links to other web sites, news articles, or anything else that the writers find interesting on the Web as well as commentary on those links or news articles. Weblogs are the online version of a diary that was kept hidden from view as a child, with the notable exception of being published online for all prospective readers to see. Weblogs differ from a personal home page in that they are created most of the time by using the various weblog programs available, such as Blogger (http://www.blogger.com) or Movable Type (http://www.movabletype.org), which make weblogs easier to maintain and create.

Weblogs come in three forms: informational (providing subject-specific information to the reader), personal (a personal diary), and informational-personal (a mixture of both). In terms of currency, users should only be interested in the informational weblogs, those that provide numerous news items, web sites, and other data. Some weblogs may start out as personal and then move over to informational (there are no hard-and-fast rules—in fact, there are no rules) or vice versa. The informational weblogs will be updated on a daily basis and will usually follow the same format throughout. Another difference between informational and personal weblogs is the language that is used. Informational weblogs will more often use language that is professional in nature as well as terminology that is familiar to the audience. Only informational weblogs are discussed in this chapter.

This chapter focuses on how to create weblogs (as having one is a useful way to stay current), provides a review of one of the programs that is used to create a weblog, addresses the pros and cons of using weblogs for currency, provides various tools that have been developed to make the "blogging" experience more inviting, reviews the major weblog directories and search engines, and discusses the weblogs available in the field of library and information science.

CREATING A WEBLOG

As mentioned, one need not use blogging software to create a weblog, but, because most people do, a discussion of the features one should look for when deciding which one to use is necessary. These features are similar to those discussed in chapter 3, on web site monitoring software, but are used in a different context when discussing weblogs. Learning how to set up a weblog is useful for those who stay current in their chosen fields, because publishing a weblog forces one to find resources on which to comment and publish in weblog format.

First, does the software need to be downloaded or does it require one to log in online? If the software must be downloaded, does it need to be constantly running on the desktop to be used or can it be installed on a web server and then accessed online? These factors may not be important to the user if one computer may be used for all blogging needs. However, for those who use two computers throughout the day and will be publishing from both, it may be difficult downloading two versions of the same software if it is purchased. I have used three different methods of blogging (logging in via the Web, downloading the software and running it each time I want to publish, and downloading the software and only installing it on a server once), and I prefer those that can be accessed via the Web, so as to be able to post from wherever there is an Internet connection. In the same vein, there may be a fee involved in using the software, or it may be free.

As with the other methods of keeping current mentioned in this book, it is important to use a weblog tool that is easy to use. Although there is always a learning curve when using any new tool, one need not spend hours learning how to post to a weblog. Weblogs were specifically created for those who do not have expert computer skills (this includes yours truly) and would be missing the point if they were too difficult to operate. To be sure, there are aspects of weblog software that need not be learned to publish a basic weblog. These basic functions should be easy enough to be able to publish within minutes of wanting to do so.

Many weblogs come with advanced features that presume to set their tool apart from the rest. When deciding on which program to use, ensure that it has specific options available. These include the automatic archiving of posts, bookmarklets (mentioned in chapter 3) for quick publishing, automatic RSS (Rich Site Summary or Really Simple Syndication) feed generation (to be discussed in more detail in chapter 5), a section for readers to comment on the posts, a spell-checking feature, and an e-mail notification list. Although not necessary in the overall functioning of the weblog, these advanced options make the published site more user-friendly and interactive.

For those who post frequently to their weblogs, the buildup of the written word can become unwieldy. Librarians are used to archiving material when storage in one section of the physical library becomes overcrowded. Sometimes it is necessary to put books or periodicals into storage (whether that is off-site or in the basement). There is a similar notion in the world of weblogs. Most of the weblogging tools will allow for automatic archiving of postings. These archives can be made available to the readers within a special section of the site or within links listing the dates chronologically directly on the front page.

Bookmarklets serve a similar function in weblogs. They allow the user to easily post to the weblog directly from the browser. Bookmarklets can be in the form of a button situated on the browser toolbar or placed within the favorite's links. When the blogger finds a news story or web site that is deemed interesting enough to post and comment on, he or she can simply click the bookmarklet to launch the weblog program and publish it. Some programs will already have the title field filled out with the link already in place. Bookmarklets make blogging a simple task and enable the writer to post quickly to the site, which is one of the reasons why weblogs are very popular.

As noted, RSS feeds are discussed at length in chapter 5; however, it is necessary to mention them here, as they fit into the weblog schema. RSS feeds are a form of XML (Extensible Markup Language) in which the content from numerous web sites (including weblogs) is taken from the site and syndicated into one format. This content can be read through a piece of software called an aggregator or displayed on a web page (although most users prefer the former). Using aggregation for currency can cut down the amount of time spent on keeping current to half of what it was in the past because all of the content you have to read is brought into one place. But, to read an RSS feed, the Webmaster of the site must have made one available. These feeds are very popular for those who read a lot of weblog content, and most weblog software programs will automatically create one for the publisher of the site.

The idea of the weblog is to be able to publish whatever the writer wants, easily and painlessly. Weblogs enable democracy to flow evenly in the virtual world. To enhance this experience, some weblog programs allow for a comments section, where readers can also share their thoughts about a particular posting. A comments section is only an option. Some bloggers do not want others to comment on their weblogs as users can sometimes become unruly and flame wars ensue. Fortunately, this option can usually be turned on and off easily by checking a button in the setup feature, and most commenting features allow the blogger to delete any comment or to ban certain people from commenting entirely. For those tools that do not have comments available within the programs, there are free commenting tools available that one can easily incorporate into the weblog, although having one within the program is easier.

For those who have a spelling deficiency (like yours truly), spell-checking programs are necessary whenever one is performing any writing task. Weblogs are no exception. When one is writing and posting to a weblog, there is sometimes so much emotion that goes into the post that spelling is not considered. Also, because many people post a lot of material on a daily basis, spelling is the last thing on their minds. Some weblog software has a spell-checking feature built in, and before publishing the information online, users can spell check their work.

The last feature that is prevalent among the weblog tools is the providing of free web space to every person who uses their software to build and maintain a weblog. Although the free web space movement was prevalent when the public Internet started to take place and has since disappeared almost to this method to attract customers to their service and have ads flowing within them to turn a profit (or hope to turn one). The customers do not seem to mind the ads and are willing to have them displayed on their weblogs, provided they get the opportunity to publish at will.

BLOGGING SOFTWARE

Because weblogs are such an important part of keeping current and, as mentioned, maintaining one is a useful means of professional development, a review of one of the four major companies that provide weblog services is in order. Although there are several weblog tools on the market (in fact, new tools pop up every day), the one that will be discussed is one of the most popular among weblog users.

Blogger (http://www.blogger.com) is one of the largest weblogging tools on the Web and has been a staple in the blogging business since August 1999 (*see* figure 4-1). As of January 2003, Blogger had more than one million registered users. Blogger does not require the user to download the software,

which means that publishing and editing the weblog can be done from any computer. If more than one computer is used throughout the day (at work and at home), one need not worry about not gaining access to the weblog as long as an Internet connection is available.

Blogger is free to use, although the serious weblog writer can gain access to Blogger Pro (http://pro.blogger.com) for $35 per year (*see* figure 4-2). Because there are so many Blogger users, the servers that house the information that allow for web access are sometimes down because of overuse. This usually happens during peak publishing times (mostly during the evening hours). Blogger Pro is housed on a different server and is not accessed as often as the server attached to the free subscription. Thus, it is never overwhelmed with too many users. One of the drawbacks of utilizing space on a company's server, especially one as popular as Blogger, is the possibility of not having access to it. Blogger Pro also has features that are not available to the users of the free software.

Blogger is relatively easy to use once the weblog is set up. One of the difficult parts is the actual setup process, especially if the user is using his or her own web domain rather than the one provided. Blogger has an affiliate

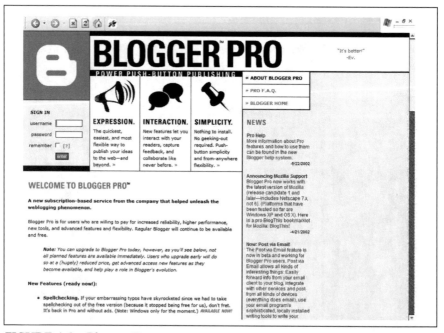

FIGURE 4-2   **Blogger Pro**

program called Blogspot (http://www.blogspot.com) in which the user can use free space for his or her weblog in return for an advertising bar on the top of the screen. If you use Blogspot, the setup will take a few minutes. If you use your own domain, there are a few extra steps to take before you can start publishing, such as pointing Blogger to the right folder and subfolder on the server that is being used, setting up the archiving folders, and having the archival information point there. For those who do not have the Webmaster skills to create an interface for the weblog, Blogger provides many choices. These interfaces are available whether the user uses the Blogspot software or not.

Many web sites have weblogs as part of their pages rather than having the entire site made up of the weblog. For example, on my weblog (http://www.librarystuff.net), I used to have a cartoon (http://www.overmedia.com) placed before the weblog postings as well as outbound links discussing other areas of my professional work. To get the text of the weblog to publish, I had to make sure that the Blogger codes that are needed to publish to the site were placed in the correct spots within my page. Users of the interface designs that Blogger provides for free need not worry about placing the Blogger codes into the weblog as they are already in place. Thus, new bloggers might decide to use one of these premade interface designs as they are truly easy to set up and use.

WEBLOG PROS

As with all software used for currency, there are pros and cons when working with weblogs. This section and the following one discuss these pros and cons in detail. In some instances, the same aspects will be beneficial to some and a deterrent to others. This is the nature of the weblog, depending on the point of view of the user. I have found that the benefits outweigh the costs that weblogs have had on information science and our quest for currency.

Some of the most useful weblogs are collaborative efforts. A collaborative weblog is one whose information is posted by more than one person (and commented on by many). Examples of collaborative weblogs include the following: Slashdot (http://www.slashdot.org), which deals with the "geeky" side of technology (with more than fifteen authors producing content every day and more comments from readers) (*see* figure 4-3), and Metafilter (http://www.metafilter.com), which touts itself as a "community of users that find and discuss things on the web. The topics run the gamut, and tend to run intelligent and civil. If it's your first time here, hang out, and get a feel for the

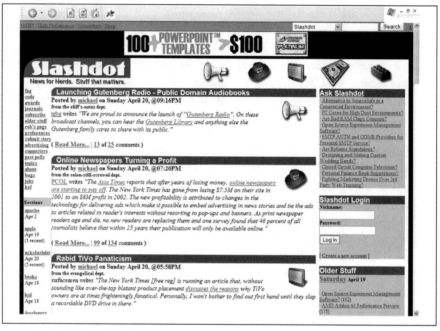

FIGURE 4-3   Slashdot

place." On any given day, there are more than thirty posts to Metafilter, with just as many comments from readers. One last weblog, among the many, that deserves mention is Library and Information Science News (LISNews) (http://www.lisnews.com), a weblog dealing with all aspects of librarianship. LISNews stories are posted by numerous parties interested in the field of librarianship, and this weblog is one of the best resources for keeping current in librarianship (LISNews is discussed further below).

Collaborative weblogs differ from weblogs posted by individuals in that they provide a community for those interested in the same topics to post stories, comment on those stories (sometime even argue), and solve any problems that may arise in their professional lives. At times, however, collaborative weblogs can become unwieldy as the many people who have the ability to post to the weblog may cause too much information to be published. The administrator of the site (usually the owner who pays for it) may have to intervene and delete posts that are "off topic."

Collaborative weblogs are important for those keeping current because they have the potential to provide both sides of any story that is posted. For example, if one person posts a story about a controversial issue and makes a comment on the post, then another contributor can provide another perspective on the same topic. I once read somewhere that to truly believe in one's own viewpoint, it is necessary to first look at the other side of the story. Collaborative weblogs allow the weblog reader to see both sides of an issue in the same place.

Similarly, most weblogs will have a link after every post that will let readers comment on what is written. Although not collaborative in nature (as only one person is doing the posting to the site), a commenting feature that allows readers of the weblog to post their thoughts on the post enables others to see other sides of the issues as well. Some weblogs do not have any commenting feature enabled, and the posts will only reflect the views of the creator of the site. This is not necessarily a disadvantage. For example, not having a comments link avoids flames (comments that are mean and counterproductive to meaningful discussion), unnecessary comments that have nothing to do with the topic at hand, and other information overload that sometimes ensues in the commenting section of popular weblogs. In fact, if one looks at the most popular weblogs on the Web (not including collaborative weblogs, which thrive on the comments) as measured by Blogstreet (http://www.blogstreet.com), a popular linking weblog directory, one would see that the top-ten individually owned and posted weblogs do not have commenting systems in place.

The subjective nature of weblogs also makes them a prime target for those looking to keep up on certain topics. Because they are easy to set up at a minimal cost, those who normally would not have a presence on the Web because of not having the skills to create a web page can get their thoughts out for all to read. Some of today's popular thinkers did not have a web presence until weblogs started to break into mainstream media. For example, Andrew Sullivan, a popular political and cultural journalist, maintains a daily weblog (http://www.andrewsullivan.com). Without the advent of weblogs, it is possible that fans of his work would not be able to read his writings every day. Weblogs also bring writers who would not normally be read in the mainstream media to the online world. In terms of currency, as mentioned in a previous paragraph, the ease of publishing to a weblog brings voices to the forefront that provide views that differ from the "typical" writers in a field of study.

Weblogs are able to provide up-to-the-minute news because they are technologically capable of being easily updated multiple times throughout the day. During the days after September 11, 2001, weblog writers were constantly providing updates on the aftereffects of that tragic day as we all attempted to deal with a situation that we had never experienced before. The weblog not only provided an outlet to deal emotionally with the events of that day, but it reinforced the notion that we live in a free society that allows for the publishing of our innermost thoughts and feelings. Also, because weblogs are constantly updated, they tend to provide news to the reader before it reaches the morning paper or other online sources, which was important after the attacks because we were all searching for answers and new information throughout the days after the attacks.

Weblogs have grown exponentially since they burst upon the scene, and one of the reasons behind this extraordinary growth involves the displaying of subject-specific information in one place. Librarians and other professionals can catch up on news and new tools related to their professions. In addition, as more people catch on to weblog technology, they begin to start industry-related weblogs as well. This has occurred in two professions that I constantly monitor: librarianship and the law. Library weblogs will be discussed later in this chapter.

Legal weblogs discussing the many facets of law have become so popular that they have spawned their own name. *Blawgs* was coined by Denise Howell, a California attorney who maintains a weblog entitled Bag and Baggage (http://bgbg.blogspot.com). In addition to her witty comments about technology and the legal profession, Howell maintains a list of blawgs broken down into subcategories for easy access. Another attorney who maintains a categorical list of blawgs (http://radio.weblogs.com/0104634/outlines/law%20blogs.html) is Ernest Svenson, who maintains his practice in Louisiana and is known as Ernie the Attorney. Svenson's list, along with Howell's, provides detailed coverage of the many blawgs that are regularly updated as well as new blawgs that are created every day. Blawgs have become so popular that a web directory has become available (http://www.blawg.org) that contains information on legal-related weblogs (*see* figure 4-4).

As mentioned previously, one of the best ways to stay current on the Web is to publish daily to a weblog. If a reader promises him- or herself to read fifteen to twenty weblogs per day and review various news resources for publication into his or her own online journal, the information read on these journals provides the necessary fodder for keeping current in the field of librarianship. Although reading weblogs alone may allow one to keep current, librarians who write weblogs may tend to get more out of the material in that they are spending more time collecting the content, analyzing the material, and putting down their thoughts about it. Posting to a weblog and maintain-

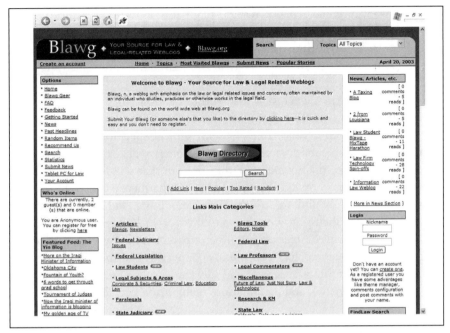

FIGURE 4-4   **Blawg**

ing a consistent web presence allow for interesting networking possibilities and other professional development opportunities. When I am asked why I spend time working on my weblog, I usually reply that I do it for selfish reasons: I want to stay current, "get my name out there," and focus on the job of being a reference librarian.

Not only do weblogs allow the professional librarian to stay current, but they can allow your patrons to do so as well. Several public and academic law libraries around the world have used weblogs to keep their constituencies up-to-date with what is happening in the library. For example, a popular site among library-weblog readers is the Waterboro Public Library, in Waterboro, Maine (http://www.waterborolibrary.org/blog.htm). Its weblog provides library users with updates on new books added to the shelves, book reviews, fiction with Maine as a backdrop, news about libraries, and useful web sites. In Wilton, Connecticut, the Wilton Library publishes a weblog (http://www.wiltonlibrary.org/weblog) for its patrons as well. Postings include the top-ten books checked out of the library, the ten most requested titles, and other related information. And finally, the Springfield Technical Community College

Library, in Springfield, Massachusetts, maintains a weblog (http://library. stcc.mass.edu/blogger/blogger.html) that details the latest programs, changes in the hours of operation, and other pertinent information useful to customers. Thus, weblogs can also be used as a marketing tool for any type of library site.

The very nature of weblogs is that, within the posts, they will link to posts from other relevant weblogs that their owners have found useful. This allows the user to build up a collection of useful subject-specific online informational journals that publish similar works. Weblogs will also have a favorites listing either on the main page or within the site that will list other weblogs that their owners read on a daily basis, adding to the theory that weblogs exist in a community. By linking to one another's posts, adding them to the favorites list, and discussing what is written by other bloggers, each member of the group becomes a trusted online companion. A networking craze has erupted within the weblog community (especially in the library-weblog world), where friendships are made and ideas are spawned that lead to articles and books being written and presentations being made at national conferences.

WEBLOG CONS

Because weblogs are usually run by those who do it on their own time, with their own money (if they choose to—as mentioned weblogs can be run for free), then there is no law that dictates when weblogs have to be updated or even stay live on the Web. The most informative weblog used in the field of library and information science can close its doors forever and not return. Also, a weblog can cease to have updated news for weeks on end if the publisher is on vacation or busy with other aspects of his or her life. This is why collaborative weblogs work better. If one person decides that he or she has had enough and will not be adding news items to the site, then there are others who will be able to pick up the slack. For weblogs owned and operated by one person, this is not the case (unless another individual takes over). There is a reliability factor existent in other forms of electronic media; for example, the online version of *Library Journal* or *American Libraries* is more likely to outlast many weblogs as each is sponsored and run by a company or organization that has been around a long time.

There are numerous examples of weblogs that have not lasted because of time constraints but none more heartbreaking than the New Breed Librarian (NBL), which was launched in early 2001 to rave reviews. NBL (http://www.

newbreedlibrarian.org) was a bimonthly publication for those new to librarianship and provided edgy articles dealing with progressive issues. Included were interviews with those who contributed to the library field, a section on technology, and an advice column called "Ask Susu." There was also a running weblog on the main page. For eighteen months, librarians would flock to the site to read the free publication plus catch up on the news via the weblog. NBL was becoming one of the more popular weblogs until its abrupt end in August 2002, the authors citing time constraints. It was a sad day in the library weblog world, and NBL continues to be missed. So far, there has not been any new NBL-type weblog to fill the void that was left.

The subjective nature of weblogs was discussed in the previous section, on their positive aspects toward currency, but there is another side to it. Too much subjectivity in an informational weblog can lead to possible confusion between content and commentary, and the true purpose of currency may be lost. Although it is important to understand both sides of any issue, the news may be lost in the commentary that is provided by the weblog writer. I have struggled mightily with this issue while working on my own weblog. How much news should I publish in relation to my commentary on the issues at hand? This boils down to the weblog readership: some readers visit weblogs for up-to-date news on a particular subject while others enjoy reading the commentary. The weblog writer determines how much commentary versus news publishing to provide on any given afternoon, and it is possible that more commentary will appear on some days than others, depending on the mood (and time constraints) of the weblog writer. Another negative aspect of weblogs that will have an effect on the professional attempting to stay current is the "anyone can do it" factor. Because weblogs can be created by anyone who has access to an Internet connection on a semiregular basis, there exists the potential for too many to exist at one time. The beginning weblog reader is forced to find the weblogs that best fit his or her needs and trudge through the ones that will not help at all in the quest for current information. Even if one finds many weblogs that will help one to keep current, there is always the possibility of information overload. Reading weblogs leads to reading more weblogs, which, in turn, leads to reading yet more weblogs, because they all point to new and exciting writings, commentary, and sources for more information. Information overload has always been a problem since the Web has become so popular, but weblogs have enhanced this exponentially. The trick to avoiding information overload when dealing with weblogs is to stay focused on the tasks at hand, to delete weblogs from the favorites folder as often as they are added, and to read only as much as your precious time will allow. I have found that reading fifteen to twenty weblogs per subject per day (which takes me about twenty minutes) is effective.

In a related matter, there is a lot of crossover in weblogs, especially those that provide news in subject-specific fields, such as legal research or library and information science. Many weblog writers will glean their information from the same news sources or even from each other's weblogs. The idea inherent in currency is not to read the same stories over and over but to gain fresh data from a variety of sources. Avoiding crossover altogether is an impossible task, but if readers find that stories in one weblog are just repeating those in another, then there is no use in reading both weblogs. One key is to read weblogs from different subcategories of the main topic. Thus, in information science, there may be a weblog that posts stories and commentary on technical services and cataloging, while others discuss e-books, and still others mention new reference sources. Although crossover of stories may be avoided, the information gleaned from reading two different types of weblogs may not suit the reader's specific needs.

Another negative aspect of weblogs is that they can become addictive very quickly, and important work may be ignored while reading them throughout the day. It is important to note that although keeping current is an important part of our profession, reading numerous weblogs (or even surfing the Web in general) should not take precedence over the day-to-day responsibilities of being a librarian. Keeping current should only supplement the work we do for our patrons, not replace it. One way to resist the addictive nature of reading weblogs (although some may not suffer from weblog addiction—it depends on many factors, including personality type) is to read them while on a break at work or at home.

The final reason why weblogs may not be ideal for keeping current is the expertise factor. Because weblogs, like any web page, can be run by anyone with Internet access, it is possible that one might purport to be an expert in a particular field of study when, in fact, the opposite is true. In fact, the information that is provided may have been found on another weblog, and the data may have been skewed. Librarians were taught in library school to use valid and well-known resources when attempting to answer a reference question and, if possible, to use multiple sources for backup. The same should be true for electronic media, especially when dealing in the weblog format, because of the commentary attached to the post. If using a weblog to gather information for professional development purposes, it is always prudent to find out a little background information on the writer. If none is provided, inquire via an e-mail or a phone call.

One day, while answering a reference question pertaining to a certain chemical, I happened upon a weblog entry discussing the effects if its fumes were to be breathed in, which was exactly what I was looking for. Before I provided the information to the attorney with whom I was working, I e-mailed the author asking him to provide me with a bio. I received a full résumé the next day, which convinced me that this person was an expert in his field. I was then able to send the information off to the attorney without having the notion that I might have given her false information.

Thus, treat weblogs as you would any electronic resource. There is a famous cartoon that appeared in the *New Yorker* in 1993, when the Web was well on its way to becoming the national phenomenon that it is today. It pictures two dogs. One is sitting in front of a computer and says to the other one, sitting nearby, "On the Internet, nobody knows you're a dog." In the best interests of the patrons who we serve and our own professional reading, make sure that the information that you gather is not only from a human, but also from a reputable source.

WEBLOG TOOLS

The increasing popularity of weblogs has spawned utilities that make the blogging experience more fun and useful for the reader and writer of these online diaries. There are too many to discuss in this chapter, but those tools that are helpful in decreasing the amount of time spent in keeping current as well as finding other resources from which to glean new data will be mentioned. All of these services are free of charge and have been around long enough to establish themselves as valid resources.

Bloglet (http://www.bloglet.com) provides bloggers with an e-mail notification system for their weblogs (*see* figure 4-5). Registration is free and easy, and the weblog operator need only cut and paste a few lines of code into the weblog, answer a few questions pertaining to access to the site, and the mailing list is set up. Every morning Bloglet gains access to the weblog's back end, scrapes every word from the postings from the previous day, and sends it out to everyone on the mailing list. The user can sign up for as many weblog e-mail notifications as is desired. The full text of the results will be sent in one e-mail notification, saving precious time for weblog readers. There are a few drawbacks to this service that need to be mentioned.

First, Bloglet will only gather the postings once a day. Although this may be perfectly fine for some weblog readers, many want to receive updates more

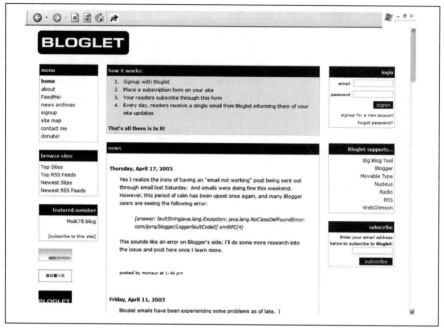

FIGURE 4-5   Bloglet

than once per day. Second, when Bloglet first came out, the only way for a user to get updates via the service was if the weblog owner had signed up and placed the code and the sign-up form on the web site. After a while, the owner of Bloglet set it up so that if a weblog provided an RSS feed, then the feed URL could be used as a substitute for the owner signing up for the service. Also, Bloglet does not work with every weblog software in existence, but its creator hopes that this flexibility will be available sometime soon. Finally, the owner of Bloglet runs the site on his own time and could decide to shut it down at any time, leaving the mailing list and all of its e-mail addresses unavailable. Even with all of these potential drawbacks, Bloglet is worth using to keep up with many weblogs via e-mail. Also, as Bloglet and RSS gets more popular, this tool will become more useful.

YACCS (http://rateyourmusic.com/yaccs/) is a system that weblog writers can add to their sites so readers can comment on the posts. Some weblog software, like Movable Type, has the commenting system already in place, but other popular weblog software, like Blogger, does not. Thus, YACCS has become a very popular tool for weblog operators (in fact, as of June 2003, YACCS had nearly 28,000 subscribers). YACCS is very easy to install in any weblog that supports the script. For those using Blogger, YACCS will install automatically into the system by placing a two-line script into the main site. YACCS is also available in multiple languages, including Dutch, German, Spanish, Italian, and French. Other features include permanent links (also known as "Permalinks") for each comment (which allows other weblog writers to link to a specific post), the ability of the weblog owner to delete any posts as well as ban users by specific Internet Protocol (IP) address (helpful for those who abuse the system), an easy-to-use system that allows the owner to change the layout of the comments section, a search option to locate specific users and comments, and the ability to read each comment via RSS. YACCS also remembers each person who posts a comment to a weblog and will automatically place his or her contact information into the comments section for the next time that person attempts to post a comment.

The benefits and drawbacks of having a commenting system in place were discussed earlier in this chapter, but there are additional aspects of YACCS that need to be mentioned. First, the YACCS comments system is used by a lot of people, and the comments are stored on the YACCS server (not the weblog itself). Thus, two possible scenarios may take place. One, the YACCS server may not be running correctly, which means that the readers and writer may not have access to it at any given point in time. Second, if YACCS is down, then access to the entire weblog will slow down as the script placed into the weblog will be attempting to access YACCS. This has happened on multiple occasions with the weblog that I maintained (when I was using Blogger). Also, as is possible with any free application, the owner of the comments system can decide that he or she doesn't want to run it anymore, and every comment that has ever been posted will be lost.

Blogrolling (http://www.blogrolling.com) allows the weblog writer to easily add another weblog (or any web site, for that matter) to a favorites list with the click of the mouse (*see* figure 4-6). By using this service, the laziest of bloggers can keep up with his or her favorites lists without having to log in to the account, access the main file, and manually insert the favorite. Blogrolling provides a bookmarklet (the same type as discussed in previous chapters) that allows the weblog writer to insert the favorite into his or her own weblog by clicking on the bookmarklet while the page is displayed on the screen. Blogrolling is free to use and works with any of the popular weblogs, and the setup is as easy as placing a few lines of code in the web site.

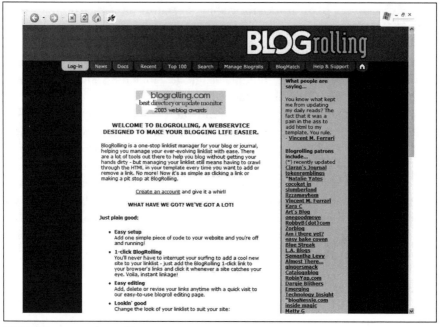

FIGURE 4-6   Blogrolling

Some features of Blogrolling include the ability to display the favorites in any format (e.g., alphabetical order, randomly, or by date and time updated); an easy way to store your favorites on the sidebar of your browser (for Netscape and Mozilla users); and the ability to manage and rename your favorite web pages and weblogs. In addition, Blogrolling has the ability to display which weblogs have linked to a certain other weblog, which enables users to find similar web sites of interest. Blogrolling is a perfect example of how a simple program can be integrated into a weblog and used by thousands of weblog operators.

There are, however, potential drawbacks to using Blogrolling. First, even though the links are displayed on the weblog, they are stored on the Blogrolling server. Thus, as in the utilities mentioned above, if the server goes down, there would be no access to the bookmarks, and access to the weblog may slow down. Also, if the owner of Blogrolling decides to take down the site, then the potential of the links to be lost is high, even though it is mentioned in the sites FAQ that the owner will send to each account the links that have been "blogrolled."

WEBLOG DIRECTORIES, SEARCH ENGINES, AND MISCELLANY

When the Web started to become a popular tool for locating information, it wasn't long before search engines and web directories became the most popular method for easily finding that information. When weblogs first started to appear, there was no need for any type of web directory, but as they became more popular and grew exponentially, weblog-only search engines and directories began to appear regularly. Mixed in with these directories are ways in which users can find the most popular links in the weblog community as well as weblogs of similar tastes and subjects.

Daypop (http://www.daypop.com) purports to index more than fourteen thousand news sites and weblogs (*see* figure 4-7). It has a clean interface and allows the user to search in "News," "Weblogs," both "News" and "Weblogs" at the same time, and RSS headlines. There is also an advanced search capability that enables the user to limit the search by the time the site was indexed in Daypop, the language of the page, and the country where the page originated. Other search functions include the link option, which will locate weblogs that link to another weblog. For example, the search string

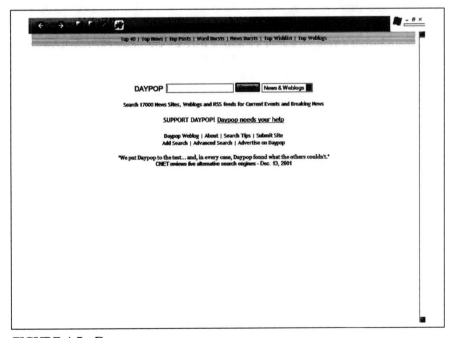

FIGURE 4-7 **Daypop**

"link:www.lisnews.com" will find the weblogs in the Daypop database that link to LISNews.

Two other popular features in Daypop include the "Daypop Top 40" and "Daypop Top News." The "Daypop Top 40" (http://www.daypop.com/top/) is a list of the top-forty links that weblogs (in the Daypop index) are linking to. The "Top 40" has become so popular that many weblog writers check the list every day to see what others are linking to and writing about. This will probably lead to the weblog being linked to by more readers, and the links will increase exponentially. If a weblog appears in the "Top 40," the number of hits for that site will increase greatly for that day. The "Top 40" list is also a way to see what is going on with weblogs on any given day. For example, as I write these words, the top-ten links in the "Top 40" deal with Google buying Pyra, the company behind the popular weblog Blogger. The list displays not only the news item, but also commentary about the acquisition from famous weblog writers.

Blogdex (http://blogdex.media.mit.edu/) is another popular weblog search engine, link aggregator, and, similar to the Daypop "Top 40," popular link generator. Hailing from the Massachusetts Institute of Technology, Blogdex calls itself the "Weblog Diffusion Index." It gathers web sites in its directory and displays them on the front page according to how many sites have linked to each site. The most popular weblog will appear on the top. Blogdex also has a simple search interface that allows the user to find weblogs with keywords in the title or the URL. Finally, Blogdex displays a link for each posting entitled "Track This Site," which shows all of the sites in the Blogdex index that linked to that URL.

Eatonweb Portal (http://portal.eatonweb.com/) is one of the original weblog directories. Comprised of just under ten thousand weblogs, this site categorizes its inhabitants into many categories, including type of weblog, languages, countries, and alphabetical. The sites included in Eatonweb Portal are added by the weblog owners themselves, and it is far from an exclusive listing. That said, there could be informative weblogs in this portal that may be helpful for the librarian (or any professional) in keeping current that are not found in any other database. For those interested in weblogs maintained by librarians, there is a specific category set aside for them. Each weblog in the database has the opportunity to be rated by the users. The higher the rating, the higher the weblog will appear on the Eatonweb top fifty (http://portal.eatonweb.com/top.php). Rating each weblog also provides the opportunity for users to share their experiences with any weblog for other weblog readers to consider. Although these rankings are truly subjective, they might

Another feature inclusive in Eatonweb is a section on new weblogs that have been added to the database. I find that to stay current using any web resource, it is always useful to locate a "what's new" or "just added" section and add it to my web site monitoring software so I can be informed of any changes to the site. The final section worth mentioning, "Resources" (http:// portal.eatonweb.com/wlm/), is a web directory of weblog resources that can help weblog writers and readers with their weblogging experience. Categories include a list of weblog directories, FAQs and definitions, hosting services, "roll your own" (a list of software that can be used to create a weblog), tools, and tracking. The resources directory alone is worth the visit to Eatonweb.

Popdex (http://www.popdex.com) is another linking weblog site that displays the most popular sites linked to weblogs (*see* figure 4-8). Each item is provided a score, which is not only based on the popularity of the item itself, but on the popularity of the sites that link to the item (this theory is one of the driving forces behind how Google ranks each site in its index). The site provides a feature that allows the user to search by news and links, just blogs, or via citations (for example, if one wants to find out what sites link to

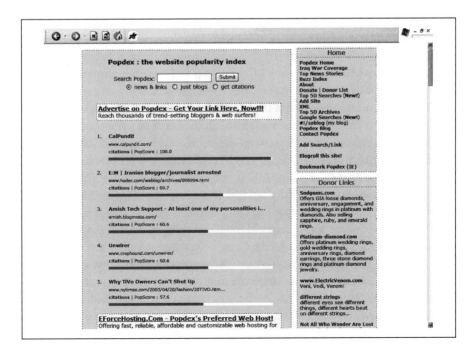

another site, then the citations search box should be used). Popdex also has a popular news results listing, which only links to sites that are found in a news resource, such as the *New York Times.*

Blogstreet (http://www.blogstreet.com) is a different type of linking weblog site in that it lists weblogs that not only link to other weblogs, but are also the most popular in terms of how many other weblogs are linking to them. The higher the number of backlinks, the higher the score at Blogstreet. Blogstreet has more than eighty thousand weblogs in its database and has a very simple interface. The first section is the blog "Neighborhood," which links to the related sites of a weblog based on the sites that the weblog writer links to. The "Blogback" feature refers the reader to weblogs that have blogrolled a particular weblog (*see* Blogrolling above). Blogstreet also lists the top-one-hundred sites that have been blogrolled, and the "BIQ 100," also called the "Blog Importance Quotient," lists the most "important" sites based on who is doing the Blogrolling. For example, if five of the top-one-hundred weblogs used Blogrolling on a site, it will score a high BIQ.

LIBRARY AND INFORMATION SCIENCE WEBLOGS

Because this book is about keeping current in the field of library and information science, I would be remiss if I didn't discuss some of the more popular library weblogs in existence today. There are too many to mention here, but Peter Scott, a longtime librarian in Canada, has put together an exhaustive list (http://www.libdex.com/weblogs.html) of national and international library weblogs. The sites that I mention here are the most popular weblogs that I have been reading for the past four years (although that may be a matter of opinion) and have been helpful in both professional development and keeping current.

Librarian.net, aka the rarin' librarian (http://www.librarian.net), was one of the first library weblogs to hit the scene (the archives date back to April 1999). Run by self-titled anarchist Jessamyn West, this weblog links to stories about librarians, sites that discuss librarians, and any other information that West finds on her daily crawl. West receives most of the links she posts from Librarian.net's high readership and determined following. The posts have followed the same pattern since its inception, with West placing her opinions along with the news and sites she discusses. In the past few years, West has begun to add quotes to the items that she posts, and readers are always enthralled by the fresh information that comes out of her weblog. The crossover between Librarian.net and the other library weblogs mentioned in this section are not a frequent occurrence, making the rarin' librarian one of the freshest library weblogs on the Web and a must read for those attempting to keep current. Those readers who like to read weblogs for reasons other than keeping current (I have at least ten such weblogs in my web site monitoring software) will benefit from reading her online journal, Abada Abada (http://www.jessamyn.com/journal/).

LISNews (http://www.lisnews.com), mentioned previously in this chapter, is a collaborative weblog created by Blake Carver, web librarian at Ohio State University. Because there are many contributors to this weblog, the postings' content is far-reaching, which can be considered positive or negative. Too many stories posted every day can become too content heavy and may lead to too much time spent on one weblog. On the other hand, the readers leave LISNews knowing that they have read at least 60 percent of the news about librarianship on one site. The beauty of LISNews is that it is constantly updated by its numerous contributors. Carver does not use blogging software to run his weblog, using instead phpSlash (http://www.source forge.com/projects/phpslash/) and his knowledge of back-end coding to run the site. There is a mailing list that users can subscribe to that is delivered via e-mail three times a week; however, LISNews is worth visiting on a daily basis.

The Shifted Librarian (http://www.theshiftedlibrarian.com) was created by Jenny Levine, the "Infomaven" and creator of what was probably the first library weblog, Jenny's Site du Jour (http://www.jennyscybrary.com/sitejour.html), which is now defunct. Levine defines a "shifted librarian" as one who receives information rather than going after it. Levine's passions include gadgets, RSS feeds, and weblogs and how they can improve the lives of libraries and their constituencies. The Shifted Librarian uses the Radio weblogging software to run the site and takes any opportunity to praise the aggregator that comes with it. This site is well worth a visit every day.

Peter Scott's Library Blog (http://blog.xrefer.com/) is another informative weblog, the only one I know of that is sponsored by a commercial organization (in this case, Xrefer). Formerly known as Library News Daily, Peter Scott's Library Blog posts links of interest for the library profession, with a focus on new issues of online trade publications, upcoming conferences, and other resources for the library professional. Besides his weblog and extensive list of library-related weblogs, Scott also maintains lists of library journals (http://www.libdex.com/journals.html) and publishers' catalogs (http://www.lights.com/publisher/). Not related to currency, but worth mentioning here, is Scott's index of eighteen thousand libraries (http://www.libdex.com/).

Scholarly Electronic Publishing Weblog (SEPW) (http://info.lib.
uh.edu/sepb/sepw.htm), maintained by Charles W. Bailey Jr., assistant dean of
systems at the University of Houston Libraries, is another weblog worth mentioning in this section (although there are many worth reading). SEPW
focuses on the open access movement and online scholarly publishing, which
have become hot topics over the past few years and continue to spawn attention. Bailey also discusses digital technologies and mentions new articles of
interest in library publications (online and off) and is also the man behind the
Scholarly Electronic Publishing Bibliography (http://info.lib.uh.edu/sepb/
sepb.html), a subject listing of articles on the same subject.

NewPages Weblog (http://www.newpages.com/weblog/default.htm)
calls itself "The Alternative Guide to New Books, Magazines & Music along
with News & Views from the Net of Interest to Booksellers, Publishers,
Librarians, Writers & Readers." Although not fully enmeshed in the field of
librarianship, the NewPages Weblog provides stories that relate to the profession, but it also contains articles that other weblogs wouldn't necessarily link to.
Thus, the crossover element is usually not a factor. Another part of the NewPages
site worth mentioning is "Uncle Frank's Diary" (http://www.newpages.com/
unclefrank/default.htm), a monthly column that usually comments on library
issues.

Other library-related weblogs include the following: **LACK** (or
Librarians Are Corrupting Kids) (http://www.conk.com/zed/lack/), published by Chris Zammarelli, links to stories on book censorship and web filtering that affect librarians and their patrons; **Inter-alia** (http://www.inter-
alia.net/) is a legal research weblog, put out by Thomas Mighell, and also has
a weekly newsletter; **BeSpacific** (http://www.bespacific.com) is another
law-related weblog posting stories on law and technology news.

Although weblogs have positive and negative aspects, they are well worth
pursuing when one is attempting to stay current in any aspect of information
science. There are plenty of informational weblogs; the trick is to find those
that are helpful while weeding out those that are not. The weblog tools listed
in this chapter will give the librarian a good start either with reading or
writing in the weblog format. As I have mentioned, one of the most effective
ways to make sure that you keep current is to own a weblog and post a few
stories to it daily. Doing so will also help you network with colleagues, gain
writing and presentation opportunities (if desired), and encourage you to
excel on the job.

RSS Feeds 5

Imagine having new content from your favorite web pages delivered to you in one list, so the only online reading that would need to be accomplished for keeping current would be to peruse that one list. Instead of working with web site monitoring software, setting up each site so as not to provide irrelevant data (and waste valuable time), and sifting through the layout of the page, only the content of each site appeared on your desktop every morning and updated itself in intervals of one hour throughout the day. What was once considered an impossibility is now becoming a reality, as RSS (Rich Site Summary or Really Simple Syndication) feeds have started to make waves in content management and delivery of information, and they are a guiding force for professionals interested in keeping abreast of what is going on in their professions.

RSS is a form of XML (Extensible Markup Language) whose content is only readable by using software called an aggregator. An aggregator (sometimes called a news aggregator) reads the XML files of web pages (which can include news sources, weblogs, and newspapers), organizes the material, and displays it for the user. The user need not go to the site to read new content, as it is brought from the site (via its feed) to the user. Whenever I discuss currency with colleagues, I always mention that I rarely go out and search for news stories, web sites, or other reference material for currency. All of the new information that I receive comes to me either from web site monitoring software or in the form of RSS feeds.

The first step in learning about RSS feeds is recognizing sites that have RSS capabilities. The most obvious way is to look for an orange button with the letters *XML* on it or a blue button with the letters *RSS* on it. Both of these buttons essentially perform the same task. These buttons are usually placed on a web site in full view, and those who understand RSS feeds will know that the information contained on that web page can now be read in a news aggregator. RSS feeds are very popular in the blogging community, and they are automatically created by the software that runs many weblogs. Radio (http://radio.userland.com), Blogger (http://www.blogger.com), Movable Type (http://www.movabletype.org), and Live Journal (http://www.livejournal.com) all automatically create RSS feeds. Not all web sites have RSS feeds, and this will be discussed at length later on in this chapter. Also, not all web pages with RSS feed capabilities will have the relevant buttons on the site, and they may be hidden from view. We will discuss this later as well. What is important to know is that to read content in an aggregator, there needs to be a feed from that site.

Recognizing RSS feeds is also important. They will usually end in .xml, .rss, or .rdf, although some feeds do not end in any of these three syntaxes. The key to locating RSS feeds is to look for the orange or blue buttons described above. Next, although they look like URLs that can be read in a browser, RSS feeds can only be read using an aggregator. As an example, place this URL in Netscape or Internet Explorer: http://www.lisnews.com/lisnews.rss. The browser will try to read the data as a web page, but because RSS feeds are not web pages, the data will not be readable (*see* figure 5-1).

CHOOSING AN AGGREGATOR

Now that the basic description of RSS feeds has been provided, we turn our attention to news aggregators, the software that reads these feeds. Like web site monitoring software and weblog software, there are factors to consider when choosing an aggregator. These include price, ease of use, availability of tech support, newspaper format, software or browser versions, the publishing of only new data, data publishable to weblogs, autodiscovery, organization of feeds, and e-mailing links from aggregators.

The first option to consider when deciding on a news aggregator is price. Many aggregators are free, but others cost between $30 and $40 per download or an annual fee. Unlike some of the web site monitoring software that was discussed in chapter 3, no software mentioned here charges per RSS feed. Don't let a price tag fool you. Even though there are fully functional aggregators that are available free of charge, the fee-based software may have extra

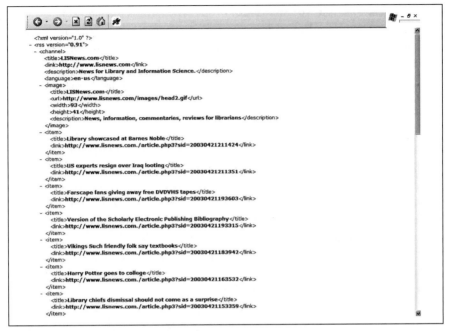

FIGURE 5-1 LISNews RSS Feed

features that make the entire RSS-aggregation process much easier for the librarian attempting to keep current.

Second, ease of use is important when dealing with aggregators, especially for those new to using them. When I first came across RSS feeds and aggregation, there was no one to explain to me how to use the software (besides spending hours using the help files). I had to play with the interface for a while before I figured out the basics behind each tool. That said, some aggregators are easier to use than others. Ask yourself these basic questions: how easy is it to add an RSS feed to the software (in RSS terms, this means that the user has "subscribed" to the content)? How easy is it to delete a feed? Is it easy to organize the feeds into hierarchical folders? Is the template easy to navigate?

Next, is tech support readily available if the user runs into problems that can't be fixed using the help index? Some aggregators are created and maintained on the side by people who have other responsibilities. There are no toll-free numbers to call if one runs into difficulties. Are e-mail addresses provided to contact the creator of the aggregator? Even better, are there online chat sessions available to discuss the issue with the creator in real time? Having tested and used four news aggregators in the past, I have found that tech support is consistently good throughout each company, but there are some that are better than others.

Because news aggregators bring all of the content into one spot, the display of such material is paramount to the user. When deciding on which aggregator to use, one should research how each feed is displayed on the screen. Does the user have to click on each headline to access the content for that particular feed or is all of the content displayed in one list? Also, within the list, is all of the content displayed under each name or is it in chronological order for all feeds, independent of the source? I am partial to the format commonly known as "newspaper," with all of the feeds to which I am subscribed laid out in one page by time of posting.

Some aggregator software products are browser based, meaning that they are displayed with the browser for easy use. Almost all aggregators need to be downloaded and placed on the desktop, which can be a problem for those who use multiple computers throughout the day (although Radio allows for remote access). Even the browser-based aggregators are not online. They rest on the desktop and use a browser to access the files. There has been an effort to get prescribed aggregators (ones with feeds already in place) on the Web, but this trend has not taken off. For an example of a web-based aggregator with the focus on legal weblogs, see the Blawgistan Times (http://clusterfsck.net/blawgistan/).

The appeal of news aggregators is that all new content is brought to the foreground without having to look at older material. This is discussed at length later in this chapter when we deal with the pros and cons of using aggregators. When deciding which aggregator to use, it is important to choose one that will only show new content. Most aggregator software builders know this to be true and have built their software in this way, but there are a few that show both new and old content. It would be ideal for the old content to be deleted from the aggregator after a certain time period, but this feature is only available in certain aggregators as well.

Because RSS feeds are popular among weblog writers, an option available in some aggregators is the ability to post directly to a weblog from the aggregator software. This way, the writer would not have to log in separately to the weblog and copy and paste any material from the aggregator into the weblog to publish the material. This not only saves time for the weblog writer, but also benefits the reader because the writer can post more information. In addition, some aggregators are only able to publish to certain weblog software, which could become a problem if you use an aggregator that doesn't have the capability to publish to your weblog.

Autodiscovery is a popular option in many aggregation software packages. Autodiscovery will automatically detect an RSS feed when a site with an RSS feed available is visited while the aggregator is in use. Thus, if my aggregator is open on the desktop and I am surfing the Web and come across a web page that has an RSS feed, the aggregator will notify me, usually in the form of a pop-up box. Autodiscovery is a great tool for many reasons; for example, RSS feeds are not always visually obvious on a page, and users might not be consciously looking for a feed but would add one to the aggregator if a feed were available.

The organization of RSS feeds in aggregators is also a key tool, especially if one subscribes to a large number of feeds. Each user should have the ability to place the feeds into hierarchical subcategories so they can be found easily and updated within each folder (so all the feeds in each category can be together). Librarians are known for their categorization and organizational skills and would use this feature on a regular basis.

Many online newspapers and magazines give the user the option of e-mailing an article to friends and colleagues, and some aggregators have this option as well. Having this option built into the aggregator saves readers time by opening up their default e-mail software and placing the post in the text box with the subject line filled out as well. The reader only needs to supply the e-mail address. The downside to this option is that many do not use e-mail software programs (or only have them situated on one computer) and thus could not benefit from it.

REVIEW OF AGGREGATORS

NewzCrawler (http://www.newzcrawler.com) is available via download for a free thirty-day trial ($24.95 per license after that) and runs directly on the desktop (*see* figure 5-2). This aggregator has an interface similar to Microsoft Outlook's, which will score points with some users for its familiar look. The names of the sites that garner the feeds are on the left side, while the headlines are on the top right. The bottom right side of the screen is a fully functioning browser that displays the content (from there one can follow links to other places around the Web). Adding feeds to NewzCrawler is easy because there is a toolbar on top of the aggregator with all of the buttons that will be needed. The interface is thus easy to navigate.

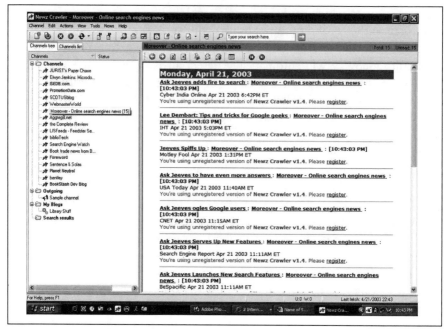

FIGURE 5-2 NewzCrawler

The user has the ability to organize each of the feeds in hierarchical folders, with the added feature of adding and naming subfolders, which is a plus for librarians who like to catalog material. By using folders to organize feeds, one can view all the new material within certain subjects at one time without searching for relevant information. On the other hand, some feeds are hard to fit into categories, as some weblog writers discuss so many aspects of their work in one place. There are feeds that are easily categorized, such as Wired News (http://www.wired.com/news_drop/netcenter/netcenter.rdp) and CNET, a technology news site (http://news.com.com/2009-1090-980549.htm). *U.S. News and World Report* now has an RSS feed for its page. Information is available at http://www.usnews.com/usnews/rss_info.htm.

I have not used the tech support for NewzCrawler, as I have never had a problem with the software, but I have heard from other users that when they had a question, an e-mail message was answered within twenty-four hours of the initial request. There are no chat sessions available with tech support, but there is an extensive help section (http://www.newzcrawler.com/online help/index.html), which can be easily navigated to assist with various issues, plus a discussion forum (http://www.newzcrawler.com/cgi-bin/teemz/teemz.pl) for users to help each other.

As mentioned, the NewzCrawler interface is easy to navigate between feeds, headlines, and content. There is also a newspaper option available that will display all of the content from each feed in a list format, according to time and date of the post. Of the aggregators listed in this chapter, only NewzCrawler has both options available to the user. The newspaper option also allows the user to see past days' postings if one is behind in professional development reading. It displays the content in html format (the common Web view) and even incorporates any pictures that are available in the feed.

The one aspect of NewzCrawler that may deter some users is its non-browser-based packaging. Even though a browser is built into the software, users may shy away from having the software constantly running on their desktop, especially if they do not use the same computer throughout the day (this is an issue with the browser-based aggregators as well). With a browser-based aggregator, one can move from the aggregator to the Web with ease without having a separate tool running at the same time, using up precious RAM. NewzCrawler also has the option for the user to publish directly to a weblog from the software and currently works with Blogger and Movable Type. The setup is easy; one just needs to know the appropriate IDs and password to access the weblog. By using the aggregator as a publishing tool as well as an RSS reading instrument, it becomes a multipurpose tool, which will attract more users.

NewzCrawler also comes with autodiscovery, in which users will automatically be notified if they are looking at a web site that has an RSS feed. If one chooses, NewzCrawler will subscribe to the feed within seconds or will pass it up. I have found the autodiscovery option a bit annoying at times because it will notify me of feeds to which I already subscribe. Thus, I usually turn this feature off. I hope that the makers of NewzCrawler will fix this issue in the future because there is a lot of potential in autodiscovery. NewzCrawler also has the option of e-mailing any post to a friend by hooking it up to the default e-mail software on the computer.

One of the nice aspects of NewzCrawler is that the user can subscribe to the RSS feed on the NewzCrawler site so that new updates to the software can be read within the aggregator and then downloaded from the site. This function is available with every aggregator mentioned in this chapter.

AmphetaDesk (AD) (http://www.disobey.com/amphetadesk) was created by Morbus Iff, a pseudonym for Kevin Hemenway, the Webmaster for a number of other web sites. AD is free for any user to download (there is no trial period), although a donation to Iff is always appreciated. AD is a multi-functional aggregator that brings all of the content from RSS feeds into one browser-based page (*see* figure 5-3).

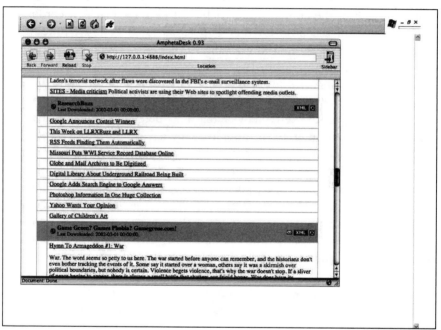

FIGURE 5-3   AmphetaDesk

There are five pages to deal with when working with AD, whereas with NewzCrawler, there was one screen. First, the software needs to grab all of the new content. A screen pops up after launching the aggregator, which displays the progress of the "syndication." This may take a few minutes depending on the number of feeds that one subscribes to as well as the connection speed. Once this is complete, the aggregator will launch the main page in a browser, which displays all of the feed content. From this screen, the user can maneuver between the remaining pages in AD, which consist of the "My Channels" page, where the user can add and delete RSS feeds; the "Add Channels" page, where one can choose from up to five thousand feeds to add to the aggregator; and the settings page, where one can set various options.

AD is built in such a way that users with knowledge of its software can add options that are not available in the official release. In fact, Iff encourages users to play with AD to create their own customizable news aggregators using the basic back end provided. A forum is available for those who wish to do this. This option is not available with the three other aggregators discussed in this book. With a customizable aggregator, users can develop their own versions of AD without having to contact Iff with possible add-ons to the software. That said, only those with advanced knowledge of Perl (the major force behind AD) will be able to take advantage of this feature. For the beginner RSS user, the basic software is quite useful.

Tech support for AD is available throughout the day, and sometimes at night, either by e-mailing Iff or posting to the AD discussion list. I have chatted online with Iff on many occasions, and he was able to point me in the right direction when I had problems with the software or with adding RSS feeds or when I had suggestions for future releases of AD. Iff has a passion for RSS and is always willing to discuss its implications and how AD can be made easier to use. The beginner user of AD will probably not have any issues using AD (as it is very easy to set up and use), so the tech support option may not be a factor. In fact, if one uses tech support for any software, that may play a factor in its ease-of-use criteria, meaning that if you have to use tech support, the software may not be that easy to use.

The content is displayed in newspaper format within the browser and displayed like a web page, with live links. If one clicks on any of the links within each posting, a new window will open with the information so one doesn't lose the aggregator. AD displays RSS content by feed title and then chronologically within each title. The titles with the most current content will be displayed on top, while those feeds that haven't been updated quite as often are on the bottom. For example, if the data from a feed from *Wired* magazine were updated at 8:00 A.M., and the news aggregator was launched at 8:30 A.M. (a common practice among RSS users—they like to get all of their news with their morning cups of coffee), the content from *Wired* will more likely be on top. Although many enjoy reading RSS in a newspaper format (which involves less clicking on behalf of the user), having all of the content from the feed provider (old and new) seems fruitless. AD winds up displaying news that may have already been read by the user the previous day. Information professionals having to read old information is contrary to this book's "keeping current" theme. Most aggregators will delete content that has already been read on prior occasions. Because AD allows users to work on the back end of the software, the deleting of posts option may already be available from another user.

The feeds' display is in one list and on a different page than the content display, which can be a problem if one wants to see quickly which feeds are subscribed to. In addition, the feeds can't be placed in hierarchical folders to the liking of the user. Only an alphabetical list is displayed with the title of the feed, a link to the XML format of the feed, and the ability to delete feeds from the aggregator. In fact, one of the more useful options available in AD is the fact that one can delete feeds from any screen.

AD does not have the capability to post directly to weblog software, nor is autodiscovery an option that is currently available. If one wanted to post data directly to a weblog, one would need to log in to the weblog back end, post the information, and then publish it. As mentioned, having these options available saves the reader valuable time in subscribing to new posts as well as publishing material on the Web. Users don't have the option of e-mailing posts to friends or colleagues directly from AD, which is valuable for networking possibilities. All of these options, although not fully necessary for using aggregators, should be taken into account if one wishes to use them.

Remember that AD is free software, and, as we have seen with these types of programs, there is a feeling of "you get what you pay for." Although aggregator makers like to please their customers with a great product, when one purchases the software, there is a vested interest in its quality from the user and maker alike. On the other hand, if an individual creates the software from scratch, he or she might be more willing to improve the software and take advice and suggestions from users.

AD is a useful aggregator for the beginner RSS user. There are no flashy "bells or whistles," but the main focus is on retrieving RSS feeds and displaying them to the user in an easy-to-follow format. The creator and regular users are always available with assistance when needed, and even though there are a few drawbacks, I would recommend it to anyone getting started in the RSS aggregator fray.

PROS OF RSS

There are always positive and negative aspects to any tool used for currency. If there were no positive traits, the tool would not be useful, and if there were no negative traits, then it would be the only tool used. As with weblogs and web site monitoring software, there are pros and cons of using RSS feeds to keep current. First, the positive forces behind RSS.

RSS feeds bring content and only content to the user. There are no advertisements, no comments from other users, and none of the other distracting material that is displayed when accessing a web site. For the user who is easily distracted when visiting a web page, RSS feeds will help maintain the focus on the content and not superfluous information.

Also, RSS feeds allow all of the content from multiple sources to be viewed on one piece of software. Thus, one need not go out on the Web and access each web site that is read every day. If these sites have feeds available, then one need only launch the aggregator, and the content will come to the user. If a web site has not been updated, then no new content will be provided in the aggregator. In chapter 1, I discussed having content come to the librarians instead of the librarians finding the content. RSS feeds are a perfect example of this theory at work.

With the librarian having less time for professional development activities because of a more demanding clientele and added responsibility on the job, RSS can get content to the user in a timesaving manner. The value of our jobs depends on how well we serve our clientele. Professional development and keeping current are just as important. By reading all of the important content for our jobs in one place, we will have more time to serve our patrons. Also, because RSS is still considered a "techie" topic, librarians with knowledge of RSS can teach others how to use it effectively. Librarians can be the forerunners in the RSS revolution.

In addition, more and more content writers are jumping on the RSS bandwagon. Popular news sites are starting to provide content in RSS format; users with coding knowledge are creating RSS feeds with tools used by librarians on a daily basis (these will be discussed later). With the addition of these top-notch back-end programmers playing with RSS, it has become a tool that will only get better and more useful with time.

Another positive aspect of RSS is the ability to display current content on any web page. This was made popular by Yahoo! and Netscape in the early developments of the Web by allowing their users to customize the information that is displayed on the screen, in essence, the development of a personalized portal. RSS can take this to another level by providing content from sites that have RSS capabilities in one place. An example in the library community is LISFeeds, a library feed portal that Blake Carver and I have developed using RSS (http://www.lisfeeds.com). When accessed, the library portal will gather content from more than twenty-five library-related content providers (from newswires to library weblogs) via their RSS feeds and display them on one page (similar to the way news aggregators work, except this program doesn't require software to be downloaded). The left side contains the feed titles, and the right side contains the content. When I click on each feed title, it will be displayed on the right side. I have timed myself reading content in the portal and was able to catch up with all of my favorite library providers within ten minutes.

CONS OF RSS

Although the positive aspects of RSS seem to conjure up thoughts of conquering the information overload inherent in the Web, it is important to recognize that RSS feeds are not the final solution (in my opinion, there never will be a solution to the information overload problem). There are negative aspects of RSS that will prove vital to any professional using the services.

First and most important is the fact that not every site has RSS capabilities, including those that have been found to be useful to librarians. Without an RSS feed, one is forced to stay current on those pages by using other methods, such as web site monitoring software or e-mail alerts (if available). Unfortunately, even though there are ways for RSS users to create feeds for sites that are not their own, an extensive knowledge of XML and other programming languages are necessary to do this. Thus, users are left to ask (and sometimes beg) the content provider for an RSS feed for their sites. Worse, the provider might not know what RSS feeds are, let alone have the time to create a feed. That said, there are tools that can be used by the provider to create RSS feeds very easily. We will go over these tools later on in this chapter.

The second negative aspect of RSS feeds is that if one uses an aggregator that is downloaded from the Web and placed on the user's desktop, it can only be used on that one computer. The user cannot access the software that has been set on one computer from another one unless the two computers are networked. This problem is especially inherent in the library field, where many librarians share the same computers at the reference desk or use multiple computers throughout the day. This issue was a concern in web site monitoring software as well—Watch That Page (http://www.watchthatpage.com) and Track Engine (http://www.trackengine.com), but these programs are based online—and it continues to be a problem with RSS and news aggregators.

A few programs have tried to fix this problem by allowing the user to export the feeds as a file, which can then be e-mailed to the user and imported into a second version of the software on another computer. I use two computers throughout the day, and I use the import-export feature in NewzCrawler and Web Site Watcher to keep both of my desktops current with each other. Although this is not the ideal solution, it is the best-known solution available to date.

Because RSS feeds are easily added to news aggregators, sometimes with the click of a button or two, it is important to keep track of the number of feeds to which one subscribes. I have always recommended to users that one should only keep up with what one has the time to do; otherwise, currency will become unruly and will only lead to frustration. At one time, I had more than 150 feeds in my news aggregator, which were built up over time, but I hardly had enough time to get through them all. Out of those 150 feeds, only 80 were truly useful to my work as a law librarian (and librarian in general). I had added some feeds on a whim but did not have time to truly read their content. One night, I performed some spring cleaning and deleted more than 70 feeds. Now, I am easily able to keep up with all of the content in my aggregator, rather than struggling daily with the time.

Another potential issue that I have seen in aggregators is that they do not have any filtering capabilities. For example, if I wanted to get content only from feeds that have the words *librarian* or *library* in them, I could not do so. As mentioned, web site monitoring software and e-mail alert features inherent in many web sites offer this option to the user, but news aggregators do not. As we have seen, however, filtering can be a double-edged sword. By including information that contains certain keywords, there is a possibility that important content will be missed, and by not filtering out content, it is possible that too much nonrelevant information will be provided. It is important to strike a reasonable balance here. Because news aggregators do not have a filtering ability available, one would need to manually filter out the unnecessary content.

USES OF RSS

As RSS has become more popular over the past few years, many have asked about its usefulness in the work environment. How will RSS help librarians and other professionals in their everyday lives? Can librarians use RSS to serve their customers better? Why should anyone bother to take the time to download aggregation software, find feeds to add, and then spend an hour each day reading the content? Even though the feeds may be available per subject, is there a way for the information to be customizable in such a way that everything is useful?

The basis of RSS is that it provides the most current information from a variety of sources. On a more advanced level, RSS can be customized to bring up-to-date information from a variety of sources to the user. Some examples follow.

First, those who use Moreover (http://www.moreover.com) to search for news know that these news feeds can be displayed on any web page by adding a few lines of code to the source of the site. Also, Moreover has set up numerous prescribed RSS feeds that can be either placed on a web page or into a news aggregator (http://w.moreover.com/categories/category_list_rss.html). Although the many subject-related feeds are a wonderful addition to RSS, every search done on Moreover can be made into an RSS feed. One need only perform a search in the Moreover engine, and add "o=rss" to the end of the URL that is created with the search. For example, if one does a search for the company Lowes, a nationally known home-improvement store, the URL for the resulting search would look like this: (http://p.moreover.com/cgi-local/page?k=librarian). By adding "o=rss" to the end of the search, it can automatically become an RSS feed and added to an aggregator. Thus, every time a new article appears in the Moreover database, it will appear in the news aggregator.

In my work environment, where current information is of the utmost importance, using RSS feeds to keep tabs on a company via Moreover has become a very useful tool. This will work for any type of search on Moreover. For example, if an attorney asks me to keep up with news on Bill Gates, I just add his name to my RSS feed. There is virtually no work done on my part (besides keeping up with the aggregator), and the attorney gets updated news as soon as it appears.

A reminder: although it is easy to get caught up in RSS, it is important to remember that using RSS in the way described above will not retrieve every article published about Bill Gates (although it will get a lot). More tracking devices may need to be put in place, such as using the Eclipse service on Lexis Nexis or using web site monitoring software on a different news engine.

Daypop (a weblog and news headline engine) has similar RSS functionality. After performing a search on Daypop (http://www.daypop.com), one need only to add "o=rss" to the end of the resulting URL to create an RSS feed for that search. Another tool that I have found useful is the creation of a keyword-specific Google News RSS feed provided by Voidstar (http://www.voidstar.com/gnews2rss.php). After performing a search in the site, a feed will be created, and the user need only place the URL in an aggregator to get updated news on the searched keyword. This may become unruly if the search is done on a common keyword, so it is important to continuously watch these feeds as they are displayed. For the librarian working in a special library, where up-to-the-minute news can make or break a deal or important case, RSS can be a savior both to the information professional and the clientele. Because librarians are content providers as well as researchers, using these feeds and getting information to the user before the user sees it will make your services more valuable to the company or institution.

In late 2002, Yahoo! quickly entered and retreated from the RSS fray by offering a feed for any public company on the major stock exchanges. Working on the "Finance" page (http://finance.yahoo.com), one could aggregate a news feed from any company by adding the sticker symbol at the end of a specific URL. Even though the service stopped days after it began, for a company as large as Yahoo! to start offering feeds showed the possibilities of the RSS revolution. If big companies start to understand the potential of providing a feed (more content views, more customers, and more profitability) to users, the legitimacy of RSS will shower upon the world. That unfortunately hasn't happened yet, but it will.

For academic librarians working on Pubmed (http://www.ncbi.nlm.nih. gov/PubMed/), an RSS feed has been created that will allow new articles for any keyword that appears in the database to be shown in an aggregator (http://www.pmbrowser.info). For example, a search for *pancreatic cancer* will retrieve the normal Pubmed results. On the results page, an orange button with *XML* on it will automatically appear. One can then place the RSS feed on that page into an aggregator, and it will be updated whenever a new article from Medline appears in the database. Of course, the full text of the articles is not available, just the abstracts. For medical librarians working in a university setting, one can easily set up feeds for any keywords that appear in Medline and show each faculty member new articles on their fields of choice. Even better, the librarian can create a newsletter of new articles that appear in the database and distribute them to professors and other professionals. This is another reasonable way (taking up little time out of the day) to distribute information and make oneself noticeable to one's clients.

In early 2003, Medscape, another academic research tool, started to create RSS feeds for subjects in its database (http://www.medscape.com/pages/ public/rss). Doctors, librarians, and even patients can subscribe to the numerous feeds available and stay up-to-date with new entries into the system. The potential for other databases, including fee-based companies, to add their content to the RSS fray is not far from reach. Imagine this scenario: using one of the fee-based databases by logging on to your library's web site, you are given the option to retrieve the results in RSS format. After performing a cross-database search, you are provided the keyword-specific feed that can be placed in your news aggregator. Whenever a new article appears in each database, you are informed via RSS. Of course, this dream is far from reality, but the potential is there.

Online newspapers are also joining in on the RSS revolution as well. Recently, the *Christian Science Monitor* (http://www.csmonitor.com/rss/) started to provide the contents of its site via RSS feeds. It has broken each section down into ten topics so the user has the choice of receiving certain aspects of the feed in RSS format. It also provides every section in one feed, but I wouldn't recommend this option as there is too much content there. For example, I subscribe to the books and technology sections. I don't have to go to the site anymore. The information comes to me in my aggregator.

As mentioned, it is only possible to subscribe to an RSS feed if one has been built by the owner of the site or was automatically generated by weblog software. For those sites that have become very popular over the past few years, I am sure that the creators have received requests to have an RSS feed available. For a non-library-related example, a few days after Dave Barry released his weblog (http://davebarry.blogspot.com/), he mentioned that many people were looking for an RSS feed. Many web site owners will usually comply with the request by providing a feed within a few weeks.

In the case of library weblogs that I have found to be useful, I have always sent a casual e-mail to the owners touting RSS and how it can bring more hits to their sites. If they mention that they do not know what RSS is and do not have the slightest idea how to provide one, I have always pointed them to the Voidstar RSSify interface (http://www.voidstar.com/rssify.php), which is the easiest way for the site owners to create a feed for their content. The owners need only place two pieces of code into their sites' back end, run it through the form provided, and a feed will automatically be created. My first RSS feed was made from Voidstar before Blogger Pro started to automatically create feeds for its weblogs.

HOW TO FIND RSS FEEDS

Now that RSS has been described in detail, including how to download and use an aggregator and customizing RSS feeds to suit the exact needs of the user, finding the feeds to subscribe to is another avenue that needs to be explored. There are three main ways to find RSS feeds. One can search via specialized search engines, use the popular engines like Google, or explore some of the weblog tools that were discussed in chapter 4, such as Blogstreet (http://www.blogstreet.com), which lists RSS feeds as well.

NewsIsFree (NIF) (www.newsisfree.com) provides RSS feeds in a search engine–web directory format (*see* figure 5-4). Users can browse for news by topic or search for the feeds using keywords. This site also creates feeds for sites that do not already have them, although there are limitations. For free, NIF will provide only five postings (there are more for that on any day) and will only display the titles. For a $20 subscription fee, every post will be displayed, plus the descriptions of each post. This site will also provide the RSS feed from the site itself, if one was created, which enables the user to use either feed (the one created by the site owner or the one created by NIF). NIF is more than just an engine and directory for locating feeds. It is also a news aggregator that will post the user's selections in a customized portal. The one problem is that only feeds that have been registered with NIF can be displayed through the aggregator. There are many feeds available that haven't

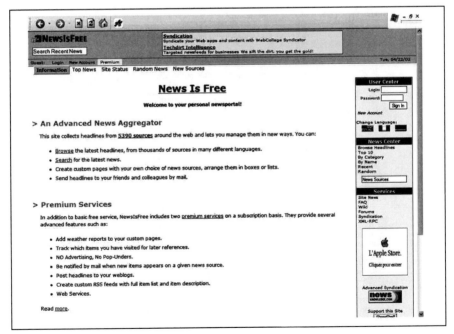

FIGURE 5-4 NewsIsFree

been entered into the NIF database. This directory currently houses more than four thousand customized feeds. Also, there is a feed available that lists new feeds that have been added to the NIF database every day (http://www. newisfree.com/HPE/xml/newschannels.hml).

Syndic8 (http://www.syndic8.com) is another search engine for locating RSS feeds (*see* figure 5-5). While NIF is a portal of feeds with an aggregator built in, Syndic8 is just an engine, housing more than thirteen thousand feeds for the user to grab and place in an aggregator. Syndic8 has also placed its feeds in four different directories, with one using the Open Directory Project (http://dmoz.org) as the subject hierarchical system. One great feature that Syndic8 provides the user is the ability to tell whether a particular feed is working. At times, the back end of RSS feeds may not be active, the coding may be wrong, or the feed may have changed URLs. Syndic8 will display to the user the last time a particular feed has been updated, which will show the user if the site has been updated and is current. For those using RSS feeds to stay current, syndicating old feeds will only waste precious time.

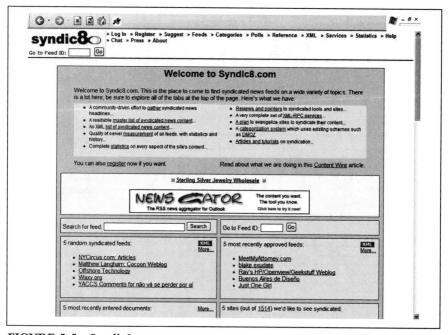

FIGURE 5-5   Syndic8

Using general search engines is another way of locating feeds, although not the best avenue. Currently, only Google indexes RSS feeds, and the user can narrow the search by having the engine look only for file types that have RSS extensions. For example, the user can locate library-related RSS feeds in Google by using the following search strategy: "library filetype:rss" or "library filetype:xml." Using these popular engines will bring up some feeds, but one would be better off with NIF or Syndic8.

One can also find new RSS feeds by reading weblogs that discuss RSS on a regular basis. In addition, to find subject-specific RSS feeds, one should read subject-specific weblogs as well. For example, in the field of library and information science, two weblogs that rarely miss new RSS feeds are the Shifted Librarian (http://www.theshiftedlibrarian.com) and Library Stuff (http://www.librarystuff.net). It is common practice in the RSS community for weblog writers to point to new feeds, sometimes before NIF or Syndic8 comes upon them. Never underestimate the power of the weblog for cutting-edge information.

Blogstreet will also provide RSS feeds for sites within the same community as other similar weblogs. For example, if one were to look up who is on the same "Blogstreet" as LISNews (http://www.lisnews.com), a list of similar weblogs will be displayed along with the respective RSS feed. If no RSS feed is available, it will not be displayed. Also, using Popdex (http://www. popdex. com), Blogdex (http://blogdex.media.mit.edu/), and Blogrolling (http:// www.blogrolling.com), one can find sites that have linked to similar items as other sites and then find new feeds from there.

RSS VERSUS WEB SITE MONITORING SOFTWARE

The question that most commonly arises when I discuss RSS and web site monitoring software in presentations and articles revolves around using both types of tools. If one can monitor any web site using Web Site Watcher, why bother reading content via news aggregator, especially if one has to download more software and learn how to use more tools? Why not place all of the sites into one tool and forget about RSS?

There are many reasons behind my argument that if an RSS feed is available to the user, one should subscribe to it. First, as mentioned before, RSS provides only content. Using web site monitoring tools, one has to manually set up the software to filter out the advertisements, dates that change every day, and other annoyances that come up when a web site is accessed. RSS has already done the filtering for the user.

Also, RSS feeds can be used to compile content onto other web sites. The LISFeeds portal could not have been put together without the power of RSS. Thus, RSS is not only a tool to use to read information; it is also a way to get information out to your colleagues and clients. Using RSS can open doors to content readers as well as content distributors, something that web site monitoring tools cannot provide.

Thus, my advice is as follows: use both tools to keep current. If a site does not have an RSS feed available, add it to your web site monitoring software, but if a feed is available, use a news aggregator. Soon, all of the sites that you want to monitor will have RSS feeds. That is how popular they are becoming. And because you've mastered the use of RSS feeds, you'll be able to use the technology successfully to help your patrons find the information they need while you keep current professionally.

INDEX

reliability of continued publication and weblogs, 60
reliability of Internet connection, 12
ResearchBuzz, 18–19
Resourceshelf, 17
Rich Site Summary (RSS). *See* RSS
Rocket News, 30–31
routing systems as print media disadvantage, 9–10
RSS, 73–92
  advantages, 82–84
  disadvantages, 84–85
  finding of, 88–91
  in Infominder, 38
  and Resourceshelf, 17
  uses of, 85–88, xviii
  vs. web site monitoring software, 91–92
  and weblogs, 52
RSS capabilities, sites with, 73–74, 77

S

Scholarly Electronic Publishing Weblog, 72
Scott (Peter) Library Blog, 71
Scott (Peter) weblog directory, 70, 71
Search Day, 16–17, 30
Search Engine Blog, 21
Search Engine Guide, 19
search engine optimization, 18, 19
Search Engine Report, 16–17
Search Engine Showdown, 17–18
Search Engine Weblog (Pandia), 18
search engines, 15–31
  evaluation of features, 17–18, 26–28
  librarians as, xiv–xv
  and locating RSS feeds, 91
  selection criteria, 21–26
  for weblogs, 67–70
search queries, monitoring of, 46
September 11, 2001, events of, 19, 57–58
Shifted Librarian weblog, 71, 91
Slashdot weblog, 55
Songfacts web site, xii–xiv
spell checking in weblogs, 52
Springfield Technical Community College (Mass.) weblog, 59–60
Steven's Theory of Currency, 13–14
subjectivity of weblogs, 61. *See also* Bias
subject-oriented web sites, 46

subject-specific search engines, 19
Sullivan (Andrew) weblog, 57
surfing the Web, 62
Svenson (Ernest) weblog, 58
Syndic8 search engine and RSS feeds, 89–90

T

technical support
  news aggregators, 75–76
  web-tracking services, 35
technologies, effects on currency of, 6
time factor
  as electronic resource advantage, 10–11
  for keeping current, 6, 13–14
  and news aggregators, 83
  as print media disadvantage, 9
tools, limiting use of, 14
Tracerlock web-tracking service, 43
Track Engine web-tracking service, 40–41
trade journals
  advantages, 8–9
  as tool for currency, 2
trademark infringement and web-tracking services, 46
tutorials on Web searching, 18
TVC Alert. *See* Virtual Chase

U

Usenet as networking tool, 3–4

V

Virtual Chase, 20–21
Voidstar RSSify, 88

W

Watch That Page (WTP), 35–38
Waterboro Public Library (Maine) weblog, 59
Web
  and currency, 4–7
  and too much information, 5–6
web directories
  for legal weblogs, 58
  and subject-oriented web sites, 46
web site monitoring software, 32–48
  costs of, 33
  evaluation of features, 33–35

Steven M. Cohen is assistant librarian at the law firm of Rivkin Radler, LLP, in Uniondale, New York. He is also the contributing editor of the "Internet Spotlight" column for *Public Libraries* magazine and creator-webmaster of Library Stuff (http://www.librarystuff.net), a weblog dedicated to keeping current and professional development for the information professional. Cohen frequently speaks and writes on the topics mentioned in *Keeping Current*. He obtained his M.L.S. from Queens College in 2001.